MICHAEL
KING OF POP

Richard Buskin

Publications International, Ltd.

Richard Buskin is a *New York Times* best-selling author and freelance journalist who specializes in music, film, television, and pop culture. He has written more than 20 nonfiction books, including PIL's *Princess Diana: 1961–1997* as well as biographies of The Beatles, Sheryl Crow, and Marilyn Monroe. A coauthor and consulting editor on the *Billboard Illustrated Encyclopedia of Music* and the *Definitive Illustrated Encyclopedia of Rock,* Buskin has contributed articles to newspapers and magazines around the globe. He has also been interviewed for such TV shows as *Entertainment Tonight,* A&E's *Biography,* E! Entertainment's *True Hollywood Story,* AMC's *Backstory,* and the *BBC Television News* and has written press releases and publicity bios for the likes of Aerosmith . . . and Michael Jackson.

Louis Weber, CEO
Publications International, Ltd.
8140 Lehigh Avenue
Morton Grove, Illinois 60053

Manufactured in China.

8 7 6 5 4 3 2 1

ISBN-13: 978-1-4508-1378-5
ISBN-10: 1-4508-1378-X

Library of Congress Control Number: 2010935740

Contents

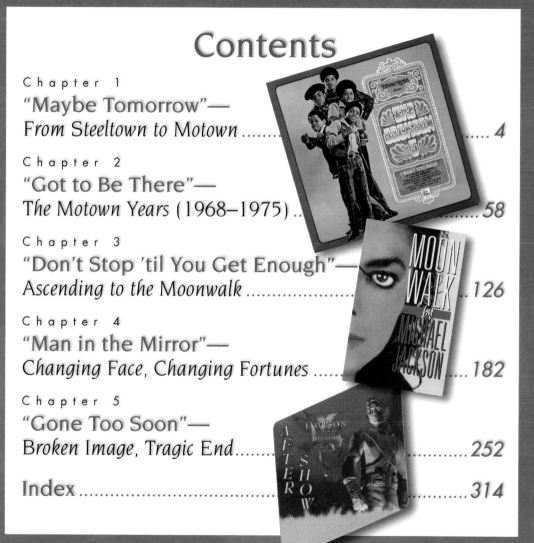

Chapter 1

"Maybe Tomorrow"—
From Steeltown to Motown

"He had it all... talent, grace, professionalism, and dedication. He was the consummate entertainer, and his contributions and legacy will be felt upon the world forever."

—Quincy Jones, Time, June 29, 2009

Michael Jackson performing at Madison Square Garden in 1981.

Vital Stats

- *Full Name:* Michael Joseph Jackson
- *Born:* August 29, 1958
- *Birthplace:* Gary, Indiana
- *Star Sign:* Virgo
- *Height:* 5'10"
- *Eye Color:* Dark Brown
- *Hair Color:* Black
- *Shoe Size:* 10
- *Occupations:* Singer, songwriter, dancer, choreographer, producer, director, actor, entrepreneur
- *Died:* June 25, 2009

Fourteen-year-old Michael Jackson, about to transition from child prodigy to all-around superstar.

Beginnings

Michael Joseph Jackson was the eighth of ten children (one of whom died shortly after birth) born to Joseph Jackson and his wife, Katherine (née Scruse), in Gary, Indiana. Joe worked in a steel mill, while Katherine was employed by a Sears department store, and music was one of their few sources of es-

cape from the daily grind. Joe played guitar in a local R&B group called The Falcons, which rehearsed in the family's tiny house at 2300 Jackson Street (coincidentally named after the U.S. president). These rehearsals had a big impact on the Jackson children from an early age, as did their mom's sing-ing and playing of the clarinet and piano. The Jackson home was bursting with music and with people. Joe and Katherine slept in one bedroom, their six sons shared a triple bunk bed in the other, and the three girls slept on a convertible sofa in the living room. It was a tight fit in a tough neighborhood, but their musi-cal bond kept the kids out of the trouble going on in the streets.

above **2300 Jackson Street—the tiny house where Michael shared a triple bunk bed with his five brothers.**
opposite **Joe and Katherine Jackson's musicality had an impact on all their kids, but Michael was always the standout.**

"I began performing at the tender age of five and ever since then I haven't stopped."

—*Michael Jackson*

Major Happenings in August 1958

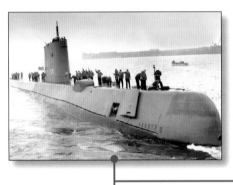

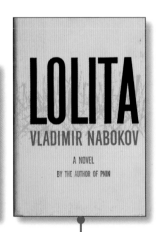

August 3
The nuclear submarine
USS *Nautilus* became
the first vessel to cross the
North Pole underwater.

August 14
Future pop icon
Madonna
was born.

August 18
Vladimir Nabokov's
controversial novel
Lolita was
published in the
United States.

August 27
The United States began
nuclear tests over
the South Atlantic.

August 29
Michael Joseph
Jackson was born.

August 30
Race riots
broke out in London.

Gary, Indiana

- *The city was founded in 1906 by the United States Steel Corporation and named after its founding chairman, Elbert H. Gary.*
- *Gary was conceived as an industrial satellite to Chicago and is located just 25 miles from the Windy City's downtown area.*
- *Gary borders Lake Michigan, which is the only one of North America's five Great Lakes that is located entirely within the United States.*
- *Meredith Willson's 1957 Broadway musical, The Music Man, featured the song "Gary, Indiana."*
- *On January 1, 1968, Richard G. Hatcher became Gary's first African American mayor and one of the first elected in a northern industrial city.*

Gary, Indiana—where the chimneys of U.S. Steel overshadowed City Hall and a family of unknowns became its brightest stars.

The Jacksons

- *Joseph Walter Jackson, b. July 26, 1929*
- *Kattie B. Screws, b. May 4, 1930 (name changed in 1934 to Katherine Esther Scruse; aka Kate, Katie)*
- *Maureen Reilette (aka Rebbie), b. May 29, 1950*
- *Sigmund Esco (aka Jackie), b. May 4, 1951*
- *Tariano Adaryl (aka Tito), b. October 15, 1953*
- *Jermaine LaJuane, b. December 11, 1954*
- *LaToya Yvonne, b. May 29, 1956*
- *Marlon David, b. March 12, 1957*
- *Brandon, b. March 12, 1957, d. March 13, 1957*
- *Michael Joseph, b. August 29, 1958, d. June 25, 2009*
- *Steven Randall (aka Randy), b. October 29, 1961*
- *Janet Dameta, b. May 16, 1966*

The union of Joseph Jackson and Katherine Scruse (opposite) *produced ten children, including Marlon's twin, Brandon, who died shortly after birth, and Jermaine, who's missing from this group photo. Back row (left–right): Michael, Jackie, Marlon, Janet, and Tito. Front row (left–right): Rebbie, Randy, and LaToya.*

Joseph Jackson

Born in Fountain Hill, Arkansas, on July 26, 1929, Joseph Jackson was raised by parents who divorced when he was in his teens. He initially followed his father to Oakland, California, while his younger brother and two sisters accompanied their mother to East Chicago, Indiana. Eventually, Joe joined his siblings in Indiana, dropped out of school in the 11th grade, and became a Golden Gloves boxer. Married for the first time around 1947, he divorced within a year. Joe then used his charm, good looks, and powerful persona to woo Katherine Scruse, whom he wed in Crown Point, Indiana, on November 5, 1949. It was while working as a crane operator at Inland Steel and American Foundries in East Chicago that he formed The Falcons with his brother, Luther, and three friends. This group earned the men extra money to help support their families, but Joe's musical dreams were never realized . . . until he discovered that his son Tito had been sneaking off with his guitar to practice playing and singing with brothers Jermaine and Jackie.

By managing them to stardom, "Papa Joe" made reality out of his kids' musical dreams, as well as his own.

FAMILY LIFE

During the early years of The Jackson 5's success, their record company's publicity machine would convey the image of the Jacksons as a happy family led by a compassionate father who was the first to spot the group's talent. Joe's sons would later reveal that this was far from the truth. Instead, "Papa Joe" beat the kids whenever they broke his rules, and it was Katherine who initially learned that Tito, Jackie, and Jermaine had a gift for music. Impressed by their singing abilities, she'd allow them to play

their father's guitar while he was at work, and all went well until Tito broke a string and was whipped by a furious Joe. When Joe calmed down and heard how well Tito could play while Jermaine and Jackie sang, he bought Tito his own electric guitar and began coaching the talented trio.

left All smiles at the Golden Globe Awards . . . but behind the happy family image there was a history of bullying and beatings. opposite Joe supporting his son during MJ's child molestation trial in 2005.

"I would get beaten for things that happened mostly outside rehearsal. Dad would make me so mad and hurt that I'd try to get back at him and get beaten all the more. I'd take a shoe and throw it at him, or I'd just fight back, swinging my fists. That's why I got it more than all my brothers combined."

—Michael Jackson, Moon Walk

Katherine Jackson

Katherine Scruse was born in the rural farming area of Barbour County, Alabama, on May 4, 1930. Stricken with polio when she was just 18 months old, she spent her school years making frequent trips to the

hospital and wore leg braces or used crutches until she was 16. The family moved to East Chicago, Indiana, when Kate was four; a year later, her parents divorced. Katherine and her younger sister, Hattie, were surrounded by music as children—

listening to country and western songs on the radio and performing in their school choir, high school orchestra, and Baptist church band. Kate even dreamed of one day becoming an actress and a singer. Ultimately, her talent and ambition (along with her Jehovah's Witness faith) were passed on to her children, including Michael, whose earliest memories were of her holding him and singing "You Are My Sunshine" and "Cotton Fields."

opposite The loving warmth that Michael enjoyed as a child came largely from his mother, with Michael and Joe in 1973 at the Golden Globe Awards. *above* Katherine, with MJ in 1988, also endowed her son with her musical talent and religious faith.

"[Michael] would act like a kid backstage, then walk onstage and be a full-grown entertainer."

—*Lionel Richie*, People, *July 13, 2009*

Older brothers (left–right) Tito, Jackie, and Jermaine stand behind younger J5 members Marlon and Michael in Chicago circa 1965.

Michael Joins the Band

No sooner had Papa Joe learned that his boys had musical talent than he spent his hard-earned cash on instruments and equipment: a guitar and an amp for Tito, a bass and an amp for Jermaine, a shaker for Jackie, bongos for Marlon, and microphones all around. Michael would watch his brothers rehearse at home and play in shopping malls, fascinated by Jermaine's singing and Marlon's dance moves. Soon he was also playing the bongos while being groomed to take over the lead vocals in a band that included Johnny Jackson (no relation) on drums and Ronnie Rancifer playing the organ. As a first grader at Garnett Elementary, Michael performed "Climb Ev'ry Mountain" in a talent show and received thunderous applause and a standing ovation. Even his teachers were in tears, and soon Michael's life was consumed with music—rehearsing with the band at home and performing in talent contests, which The Jackson Brothers started winning when Michael was just six years old. To make them sound a little more modern, the brothers soon changed the group's name to The Jackson 5.

Once Michael began fronting The J5, they were on the fast track to fame and fortune. Here, the group is pictured after winning the Annual Talent Search at Gilroy Stadium in Gary, Indiana.

Childhood Songs

"You Are My Sunshine" by Ray Charles

"Tobacco Road" by The Nashville Teens

"Cloud Nine" by The Temptations

"The Tracks of My Tears" by Smokey Robinson & The Miracles

TOBACCO ROAD

Words and Music by JOHN D. LOUDERMILK

Recorded by **THE NASHVILLE TEENS** on DECCA F11 93

SOUTHERN MUSIC PUBLISHING CO., LTD., 8, Denmark St. London W.C.2.

Even as a child, Michael had eclectic musical tastes, ranging from a nostalgic standard covered by Ray Charles (opposite, left) and the British pop sounds of the ironically named Nashville Teens (above) to a slice of psychedelic soul by The Temptations (opposite, right) and a Motown classic by The Miracles (right).

Early Musical Influences

"When I saw him move,

I was mesmerized.

I've never seen a performer perform like James Brown, and right then and there I knew that that was what I wanted to do for the rest of my life."

—*Michael Jackson, at James Brown's memorial service, December 31, 2006*

Michael appropriated the dance moves and dramatic postures of Sammy Davis Jr., Jackie Wilson, and James Brown (right)— who personally taught him how to drop the microphone and then catch it before it hit the stage. He also admired the choreographic innovations of Bob Fosse and Gene Kelly and how Smokey Robinson wrote and produced his own material.

Jackie Wilson

The Temptations

--- Smokey Robinson

Sammy Davis Jr. ----

---Gene Kelly

Bob Fosse

The Jackson Brothers and The Jackson 5

- In 1964 Jackie, Tito, and Jermaine formed The Jackson Brothers with friends Reynaud Jones on guitar and Milford Hite on drums.
- Marlon and Michael joined the following year.
- Michael's voice and dance moves helped the group win a talent contest in 1965 at Jackie's Roosevelt High School, performing The Temptations' hit "My Girl." It was around this time that Jones and Hite were replaced by Johnny Jackson and Ronnie Rancifer.
- The Jackson 5 name was suggested to Joseph by talent agent Evelyn LaHaie when she booked the group to perform in a fashion show called the "Tiny Tots' Back-to-School Jamboree" at the Big Top department store in Gary. This was on Sunday, August 29, 1965— Michael's seventh birthday.

Although unrelated to (clockwise from bottom left) Marlon, Tito, Jackie, Jermaine, and Michael, drummer Johnny Jackson is front and center in this 1966 publicity portrait.

Small Venues

The fledgling Jackson 5 performed in talent contests and small shows all over the Midwest and Northeast. These included Mr. Lucky's nightclub in Gary; the Regal Theater, the Peppermint Lounge, and High Chaparral Club in Chicago; and a variety of Midwestern strip joints. Some of the songs the group performed at these venues were "My Girl" by The Temptations, "Who's Lovin' You" by Smokey Robinson, and Joe Tex's "Skinny Legs and All."

In June 2003, Michael enjoyed a trip down memory lane when visiting Roosevelt High School (above) and other spots in his hometown of Gary, Indiana. However, some of the Midwestern haunts where The J5 had played years before were no longer around, such as nearby Chicago's Regal Theater (opposite). This had closed in 1968, five years before its demolition and transformation into a parking lot.

"When I found out that my kids were interested in becoming entertainers, I really went to work with them. . . . When the other kids would be out on the street playing games, my boys were in the house working—trying to learn how to be something in life."

—Joseph Jackson, Time, March 19, 1984

Papa Joe, Manager

After Joseph Jackson invested in the instruments, equipment, and outfits for his boys to perform with, he rehearsed them constantly, secured them gigs, drove them to and from the engagements, and behaved like an unrelenting, often brutal taskmaster—which he was. "I rehearsed them . . . every day for at least two or three hours," said Joe in a March 19, 1984, *Time* article. "He would rehearse us with a belt in his hand," Michael has said in various interviews. However, Michael also noted that his father was sure to always look out for the group's best interests, financially and otherwise. Fortunate to be among the few child artists to enter adulthood with money, real estate, and other investments, the Jackson kids were pushed by Joe to get involved in the business side of the entertainment industry, such as writing and producing music, to further secure their success.

Joe's in control: Part-manager, part-taskmaster, the Jacksons' patriarch ruled his kids with an iron fist (sometimes quite literally), but he always looked out for their best interests.

"There were times when he'd come to see me, I'd get sick. I'd start to regurgitate."

—Michael Jackson, in a 1993 Oprah Winfrey TV interview

"I didn't know he was 'gurgitatin, but if he did 'gurgitate, he 'gurgitated all the way to the bank."

—Joseph Jackson, 1993

Protective father and unrelenting manager Joe Jackson at a Jackson 5 appearance in Japan in 1973.

Harlem's Apollo Theater

- *New York's Apollo Theater at 253 West 125th Street in Harlem, New York, is listed on the National Register of Historic Places.*
- *The venue's famed "amateur night" commenced there in 1934.*
- *Associated almost exclusively with African American performers, the Apollo first hosted white musical acts in 1956, and Buddy Holly performed there the following year. Since then, others to appear at the venue have included John Lennon, Hall & Oates, The Strokes, and Björk.*
- *Among the artists whose careers were launched at the Apollo are Billie Holiday, Ella Fitzgerald, James Brown, Jimi Hendrix, The Supremes, Marvin Gaye, Gladys Knight and the Pips, Stevie Wonder, Aretha Franklin, The Isley Brothers, Ben E. King . . . and The Jackson 5.*

The Apollo Theater has a long-standing reputation for showcasing African American and Latino performers. So it's incredible to think that people of color were not even allowed to be part of the audience when it first opened as Hurtig and Seamon's New Burlesque Theatre in 1914.

SPOTLIGHT ON

The J5's Apollo Debut

In August 1967, after winning three straight amateur night contests at the Regal Theater in Chicago and opening there for Gladys Knight and the Pips, The Jackson 5 entered the biggest of all talent shows at the Apollo in New York City's Harlem neighborhood. Because their reputation preceded them, they skipped the preliminary competitions and appeared in the prestigious "Superdog" final. For the Apollo performance, Michael drew upon his experience of standing in the wings of various venues and studying every twist and turn of the acts for whom The Jackson 5 had opened on the so-called "chitlin' circuit." These included James Brown, Jackie Wilson, Sam and Dave, and The O'Jays—all of whose photos were on the corridor walls at the Apollo. The Jackson 5 not only won the amateur night contest but brought the house down—no small feat considering the Apollo's notoriously tough audience.

By the time this portrait was taken circa 1968, The J5 were old pros, having opened for popular African American performers of the time and having won the Apollo's amateur night contest.

I will alway love you"
The Jackson Five

Steeltown Records

After winning a talent contest at Beckman Junior High in Gary, The Jackson 5 were signed to a short-term deal with Steeltown Records, a local label owned by Gordon Keith who, like Joe Jackson, was a mill worker with a love of music. On a Saturday morning in early 1968, father and sons showed up at Keith's studio in downtown Gary, and The Jackson 5 laid down some tracks. The recording session was the first to showcase Michael's voice. More numbers were taped over the next few Saturdays, including one on which Joe played his guitar—the only time he ever recorded with his boys. The results were the singles "Big Boy"/"You've Changed" and "We Don't Have to Be Over 21 (to Fall in Love)"/"Jam Session." None of the songs were successful, and the master tapes were subsequently lost. But in 1994, family friend Ben Brown rediscovered "Big Boy" in his mother's kitchen pantry and reissued it the following year on the Inverted Records label.

opposite Ten-year-old Michael Jackson performing with his brothers at a festival in Gary, Indiana, in 1969. left A rare copy of The J5 single "Big Boy."

"Being onstage is **magic.** You feel the energy **all over** your body."

—*Michael Jackson*

Childhood Movies

The Wizard of Oz (1939), - - - starring Judy Garland, Ray Bolger, Jack Haley, Frank Morgan, Billie Burke, and Margaret Hamilton. Directed by Victor Fleming.

Pinocchio (1940), featuring the voices of Dickie Jones, Christian Rub, and Cliff Edwards. Directed by Ben Sharpsteen and Hamilton Luske.

Michael had a special fondness for escapist fantasies like The Wizard of Oz *(above) and entertainment blockbusters such as* The Sound of Music *(opposite, bottom). In fact, his love of* Peter Pan *(opposite, top) would manifest itself in his private life at the Neverland Ranch and in his public persona as the boyish man who never wanted to grow up.*

Peter Pan (1953), featuring ----- the voices of Bobby Driscoll, Kathryn Beaumont, and Hans Conreid. Directed by Hamilton Luske, Clyde Geronimi, and Wilfred Jackson.

--- *The Sound of Music* (1965), starring Julie Andrews, Christopher Plummer, and Eleanor Parker. Directed by Robert Wise.

Motown Records

- The Motown Record Corporation was founded in April 1960 by Berry Gordy Jr. It was his second label, following the launch of Tamla Records in January 1959.

- Motown, a portmanteau of "motor" and "town," is the nickname for Detroit, America's automotive center.

- Motown was the first African-American-owned label to feature black artists who achieved crossover success in the white market.

- The soul-based, pop-flavored "Motown Sound" became world famous during the mid-Sixties thanks to the company's remarkable in-house stable of artists, session musicians, and composer-producers.

- Motown relocated its operations to Los Angeles in 1972, and in 1988 Gordy sold his ownership stake to MCA and Boston Ventures for $61 million.

Hitsville U.S.A. (opposite), the home of Motown Records and early hits such as "Shop Around" (above). Released in September 1960 on the Tamla label and credited to "The Miracles (featuring Bill 'Smokey' Robinson)," this was the company's first No. 1 on Billboard's R&B singles chart as well as its first million-selling record.

Motown's Top Artists and Producers

Smokey Robinson

Marvin Gaye

The Supremes

The Four Tops

*Acts such as Marvin Gaye (above),
The Supremes (top right), and
The Four Tops (right) were among
the chief purveyors of the classic
"Motown Sound," melding a vibrant
and melodic brand of soul music
with gospel-laced vocals and
sophisticated pop productions.*

The Temptations

Stevie Wonder

Norman Whitfield ----------
(producer)

Holland-Dozier-Holland
   (composer-producers)

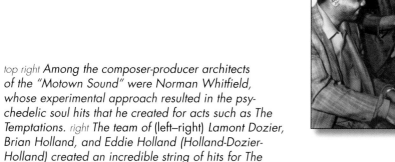

top right **Among the composer-producer architects
of the "Motown Sound" were Norman Whitfield,
whose experimental approach resulted in the psy-
chedelic soul hits that he created for acts such as The
Temptations.** *right* **The team of (left–right) Lamont Dozier,
Brian Holland, and Eddie Holland (Holland-Dozier-
Holland) created an incredible string of hits for The
Supremes, Martha & the Vandellas, and The Four Tops.**

"I first met Michael when I was in Detroit. . . . He must have been around nine or ten then, and I definitely felt that **he would be someone.** You heard the voice, and all he could do was grow. And that's what he did."

—*Stevie Wonder,* Time, *June 29, 2009*

Stevie Wonder at his piano in 1968, the year The Jackson 5 joined Motown.

The Motown Audition

■ *It was while opening for Bobby Taylor and the Vancouvers at Chicago's High Chaparral Club in July 1968 that The Jackson 5 were recommended by Taylor to Ralph Setzer, the head of Motown's creative department and legal division. This was after Gladys Knight had already arranged for some of the label's execs to attend a J5 show at Chicago's Regal Theater.*

■ *Joe Jackson canceled the group's musical appearance on* The David Frost Show *in New York City after Bobby Taylor persuaded him to have his boys audition for Motown in Detroit.*

■ *Because Berry Gordy was in Los Angeles, The Jackson 5's audition was filmed and then sent to him.*

■ *The songs performed were James Brown's "I Got the Feeling," The Nashville Teens' "Tobacco Road," and Smokey Robinson's "Who's Loving You."*

From Steeltown to Motown

2300 Jackson Street—Michael's childhood home, at an address named not after him but after the seventh president of the United States.

2300 Jackson Street, Gary

Roosevelt High School, Gary

Big Top department store, Gary

Mr. Lucky's nightclub, Gary

Gary's Roosevelt High School was where The Jackson 5 won an early talent contest, performing The Temptations' "My Girl."

Regal Theater, *Chicago* -----

Apollo Theater, *New York City*

Beckman Junior High, *Gary*

Steeltown Records, *Gary*

High Chaparral Club, *Chicago*

Motown Records, *Detroit*

Chicago's Regal Theater in 1953.

Hitsville U.S.A. at 2648 West Grand Boulevard in Detroit.

Berry Gordy

Born in Detroit on November 28, 1929, Berry Gordy Jr. dropped out of school in the 11th grade to become a professional boxer. After being drafted by the U.S. Army and serving in Korea from 1950 to 1953, he began pursuing his interest in music. A meeting with singer Jackie Wilson led to Gordy cowriting Wilson's hit single "Reet Petite" in 1957, the same year Gordy discovered Smokey Robinson & The Miracles. During the next two years he penned several more songs for Wilson, including "Lonely Teardrops." In 1959, encouraged by Robinson, Gordy borrowed $800 from family members to create Tamla Records, which would subsequently release material by everyone from The Miracles and Marvin Gaye to The Supremes and Little Stevie Wonder. Then, in 1960, Gordy formed the parent Motown Record Corporation that was based, along with its recording studio, in a house at 2648 West Grand Boulevard— the spot that would soon come to be known as Hitsville U.S.A.

Despite the smart look and smooth demeanor, Berry Gordy epitomized hard work and high expectations as the founder and head of Motown Records.

"This little kid had an incredible knowingness about him. He sang with such feeling and inspiration. Michael had a quality that I couldn't completely understand, but we all knew he was special."

—Berry Gordy, MJ's memorial service, July 7, 2009

Berry Gordy was one of two people (the other being Elizabeth Taylor) recognized by Michael and his family at The Jackson Family Honors gala and fund-raising event in 1994.

Chapter 2

"Got to Be There"—
The Motown Years
(1968–1975)

"Our parents taught us to always **be respectful** *and, no matter what you do, to give it* **everything you have.**"

—Michael Jackson, USA Today, 2001

MJ giving his all during a performance circa 1975.

Hitsville U.S.A.

After Berry Gordy's 1959 purchase of the house at 2648 West Grand Boulevard, the former photographic studio was converted into his home, Motown's administrative headquarters, and a recording studio. Located in the back of the property, the studio where many of the label's classic hits were recorded had a hole cut in the ceiling to serve as an echo chamber—an effect that can be heard on many of the early Motown records. Another property a couple of doors down at 2644 West Grand Boulevard housed Motown's Jobete Music

publishing division. The Golden World Records facility at 3246 West Davison (about four miles away) was purchased in 1968 and became the company's Studio B. That same year Gordy relocated to Los Angeles. It was there, in his new Hitsville West studio at 7317 Romaine Street in West Hollywood, that The Jackson 5 recorded their early hits . . . after passing their audition with Motown and being released from their Steeltown Records contract. Since 1985 the original Detroit headquarters has been the site of the Motown Historical Museum, run by Berry's sister Esther Gordy Edwards.

above Stevie Wonder and Marvin Gaye enjoy time together in the Hitsville U.S.A. studio during the mid-1960s. *opposite* The company's family atmosphere was never recaptured at the Motown facility in Los Angeles.

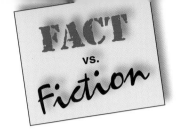

J5 HISTORY

While The Jackson 5 were recording their first album in the summer of 1969, Berry Gordy directed Motown's marketing team to concoct a warm and fuzzy biography that did more than just toy with the facts. Describing unrelated band members Johnny Jackson and Ronnie Rancifer as cousins of the Jacksons, it also tried to impress the public and the press by shaving two years off each group member's age and stating that, instead of being recommended to Motown by Gladys Knight and Bobby Taylor, the group had been discovered by the label's then-biggest star, Diana Ross. The meeting, according to legend, had taken place at a benefit concert in Gary, Indiana, during which Ross had supposedly been introduced to her "protégés" by Mayor Richard G. Hatcher. In truth, Ross first met the group when they performed at a 1968 holiday party at Gordy's Detroit mansion *after* they'd signed with Motown. Still, she did champion their cause, and Michael and Marlon lived with Ross before the family acquired its own home in California.

Miss Ross and her "protégés": Accounts of how Diana Ross discovered The Jackson 5 are fictionalized, though she did mentor the group from early on.

Introducing . . . The Jackson 5!

On August 11, 1968, Diana Ross formally introduced The Jackson 5 to 300 of her and Berry Gordy's closest friends, as well as industry insiders and influential members of the press, when they performed at an exclusive Beverly Hills club called The Daisy. Five days later she and the Supremes appeared onstage with the Jacksons at the L.A. concert venue The Forum, and that October the group made its debut before a national television

audience when Ross hosted *The Hollywood Palace*. All the while, Michael lived with Ross in her Hollywood Hills home, where she coached him on his singing and starlike demeanor and infused him with an appreciation for the finer things in life, such as art.

above **The names of legends such as record producer Phil Spector and movie director Alfred Hitchcock had both appeared above album and film titles, but it was highly unusual for an uninvolved singer to enjoy the same status.** *right* **Ross and Jackson's fondness for one another comes through on this shot, circa 1980.**

"I used to just sit in the corner and watch the way she moved. She was art in motion."

—*Michael Jackson on Diana Ross*

Childhood Movie Stars

Charlie Chaplin

Shirley Temple

Judy Garland

The Three Stooges

Shirley Temple

Charlie Chaplin

Judy Garland

The Three Stooges

Even as a child, Michael loved old movies, and this was reflected in his favorite stars, whose peak eras were the 1920s (Charlie Chaplin), 1930s (Shirley Temple), and 1940s (The Three Stooges).

"I Want You Back"

Having discovered The Jackson 5, Bobby Taylor was asked to produce their first recordings at Hitsville U.S.A. These included a cover of Smokey Robinson & the Miracles' "Who's Lovin' You," which ended up as the B-side of The J5's first Motown single. Still, it was the infectious A-side, "I Want You Back," that established their template for success. The hit was written and produced by The Corporation—an in-house team comprising Berry Gordy, Freddie Perren, Alphonzo "Fonce" Mizell, and Deke Richards. Originally composed for Gladys Knight and titled "I Want to Be Free," the adult-themed song was handed to The J5 and preteen Michael, who rehearsed and recorded it multiple times before it met with Gordy's approval. The cost was significantly more than what Motown typically spent to produce a single, but, following its October 1969 release, "I Want You Back" sold more than two million copies in America and became the group's first chart topper.

Tito, Marlon, Michael, Jackie, and Jermaine have all the right moves during an early TV appearance.

La-La Land

In August 1969, while Janet, Randy, LaToya, and their mom remained in Gary until success was assured, Joe and The Jackson 5 complied with Berry Gordy's request for them to relocate to Los Angeles. They initially resided in the seedy surroundings of the Tropicana Motel on Santa Monica Boulevard, where Michael, Marlon, and Jermaine shared one room; Tito and Jackie were in another; and Joe had a room all to himself. Next, they were guests of the Hollywood Motel opposite Hollywood High School, before Joe, Jermaine, Jackie, and Tito moved into Berry's home while Michael and Marlon lived with Diana Ross. Toward the end of 1969, after "I Want You Back" had topped the Billboard Hot 100, a four-bedroom Mediterranean-style house was finally leased for the entire family at 1601 Queens Road in West Hollywood; it boasted a living room twice the size of the family's former Gary home. Seven months later, the Jacksons moved into a larger leased property on Bowmont Drive above Coldwater Canyon.

"Come on in!" Diana Ross served as a surrogate mom to both Michael and Marlon at her Hollywood Hills home in 1969.

"I like show business, Hollywood, and all that stuff, the things people like Berry Gordy do to make you look good. I'm real excited about things."

—*Michael Jackson, 1969*

JUST *the* Facts

School vs. The Biz

■ In the sixth grade, Michael sporadically attended Hollywood's Gardner Street Elementary School while coping with his musical commitments and public recognition.

■ In the seventh grade, he attended Emerson Junior High for a grand total of two weeks.

■ Thereafter, he was privately tutored by Rose Fine, who eventually awarded him his high school diploma despite what appeared to be minimal formal education.

October 11, 1989—MJ attends the dedication ceremony for the assembly hall at L.A.'s Gardner Street Elementary School to be renamed the Michael Jackson Auditorium.

Childhood TV Shows

The Brady Bunch

The Flip Wilson Show

The Road Runner Show

Michael's tastes in TV comedy ranged from the familial (The Brady Bunch) to the slightly more outrageous (The Flip Wilson Show).

"ABC"

Faced with the difficult task of following The J5's chart-topping debut, "I Want You Back," The Corporation's Deke Richards made the chords of that song's chorus the basis of the next single. Then, playing those chords on an electric piano at the apartment of his colleagues Fonce Mizell and Freddie Perren, he came up with the line "A, B, C," followed by "One, two, three; Do, re, mi," and—surprise, surprise—"You and me." Shortly afterward, all three men were in Hitsville West recording "ABC" with The Jackson 5. Michael would later say that he preferred this high-energy bubblegum number to "I Want You Back," especially the part where he got to say, "Siddown girl! I think I *love* you!" Apparently, the public agreed. Following its February 1970 release, "ABC" sold even more copies than the group's first single and displaced The Beatles' "Let It Be" at the top of the Billboard Hot 100.

One of The Jackson 5's signature songs, "ABC" was the siblings' second No. 1 single following the chart-topping success of "I Want You Back." They performed both songs on a May 1970 episode of The Ed Sullivan Show.

In the Headlines

It was one thing to appear on the cover of African American magazines such as Ebony (opposite, right), but back in the early 1970s it was far more unusual for black artists to be accorded the same kind of exposure by journals geared toward the predominantly white mainstream market. Nevertheless, from a family feature in Life (opposite, left) to Michael's smiling face helping to sell an installment of the Story of Pop encyclopedia (right), The J5 bucked the trend and paved the way for other black acts to follow in their wake.

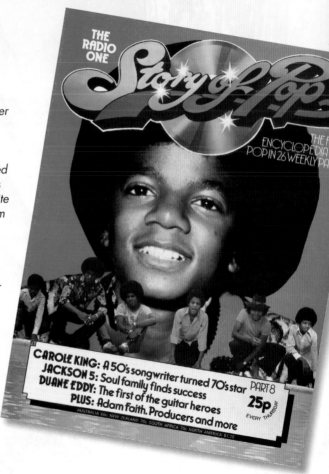

THE RADIO ONE

Story of Pop

THE F...
ENCYCLOPEDIA C
POP IN 26 WEEKLY PAR...

CAROLE KING: A 50's songwriter turned 70's star
JACKSON 5: Soul family finds success
DUANE EDDY: The first of the guitar heroes
PLUS: Adam Faith. Producers and more

PART 8

25p
EVERY THURSDAY

AUSTRALIA 66c; NEW ZEALAND 70c; SOUTH AFRICA 70c; NORTH AMERICA $1.25

"I'm gonna make you kids the biggest thing in the world. You're gonna have three number one hits in a row. They're gonna write about you kids in history books. So get ready, 'cause it's coming."

—Berry Gordy, 1968

Stars on the rise (clockwise, from top left): *Tito, Marlon, Jackie, Michael, and Jermaine, circa 1971.*

"The Love You Save"

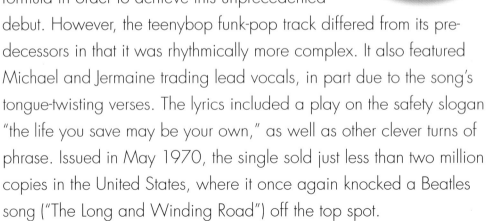

Having predicted that The Jackson 5 would start life at Motown with three number one hits in a row, Berry Gordy delivered on his promise with the release of "The Love You Save." The Corporation adhered to the now tried-and-trusted composing/production formula in order to achieve this unprecedented debut. However, the teenybop funk-pop track differed from its predecessors in that it was rhythmically more complex. It also featured Michael and Jermaine trading lead vocals, in part due to the song's tongue-twisting verses. The lyrics included a play on the safety slogan "the life you save may be your own," as well as other clever turns of phrase. Issued in May 1970, the single sold just less than two million copies in the United States, where it once again knocked a Beatles song ("The Long and Winding Road") off the top spot.

"The Love You Save" was The Jackson 5's third consecutive chart-topping single and, as written by The Corporation, was designed to help showcase the band's onstage dance moves.

JUST the Facts

The Jackson 5ive
Cartoon Series

- The Jackson 5ive *was broadcast by ABC on Saturday mornings from September 11, 1971, to September 1, 1973, and rebroadcast in 1984 and 1985.*

- *Animated mainly in a London studio, as well as one in Spain, each episode featured two songs by The Jackson 5 or, during the second season (when the series was called* The New Jackson 5ive Show*), from Michael's solo album* Got to Be There.

- *The show's theme song was a medley of The J5's "I Want You Back," "The Love You Save," "ABC," and "Mama's Pearl."*

- *Neither the Jackson brothers nor Berry Gordy contributed their own speaking voices to their cartoon characters, though Diana Ross did speak her lines in the first episode.*

- *Sometimes the animation was interspersed with live footage of The Jackson 5 onstage.*

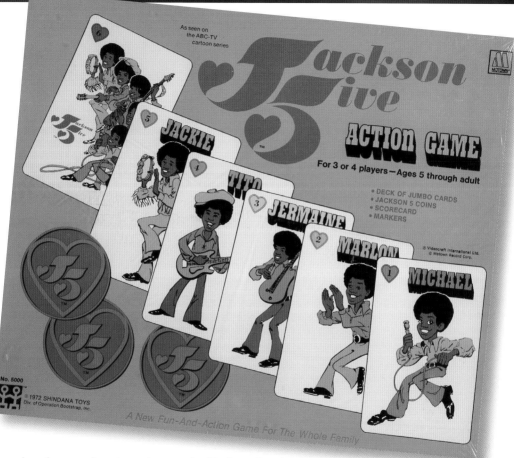

Based on the group's animated series, the "Jackson 5ive Action Game" was produced by Shindana Toys, a Los Angeles–based company that marketed ethnically correct African American dolls and board games as a means of raising black consciousness and improving self-esteem.

"I'll Be There"

Berry Gordy strayed from the hit formula for The J5's fourth Motown single, "I'll Be There." He hired writer-producers Hal Davis, Willie Hutch, and Bob West to craft a ballad that would become the label's most successful single in the United States until the 1981 Diana Ross/Lionel Richie duet "Endless Love." Michael and Jermaine again shared lead vocal duties on the track. MJ was helped along vocally by Suzee Ikeda, who was known for her behind-the-scenes work with both him and The Temptations. However, it was Gordy who encouraged Michael to echo Levi Stubbs's "Just look over your shoulder" comment from The Four Tops' 1966 smash "Reach Out (I'll Be There)." Released in August 1970, "I'll Be There" was the group's most successful single, selling more than four million copies in the United States, where it was No. 1 for five weeks. It was also the group's final chart topper.

"In the years he was with Motown, I produced Michael more than anyone. But I'm telling you, there's nothing but **sheer brilliance** on those vocal tracks. He came singing like an angel—and left singing even better."

—*Hal Davis*

According to allmusic.com, "I'll Be There," The J5's most successful single and final chart topper, "showcased the preternatural brilliance of Michael Jackson. . . . Rarely, if ever, had one so young sung with so much authority and grace, investing this achingly tender ballad with wisdom and understanding far beyond his years."

JUST the Facts

4641 Hayvenhurst Avenue

- In February 1971, Joseph and Katherine Jackson purchased a large six-bedroom, five-bathroom house at 4641 Hayvenhurst Avenue in Encino, California, for $250,000.

- Encino, which means "evergreen" in Spanish, is located in a hilly part of L.A.'s San Fernando Valley.

- The home initially accommodated the entire family, along with J5 drummer Johnny Jackson and keyboardist Ronnie Rancifer.

- Situated on two acres, the gated estate also came with a guesthouse, playhouse, servants' quarters, Olympic-sized swimming pool, basketball half court, badminton court, and archery range.

- Soon the walls of the family room were adorned with Jackson 5–related plaques and photos, as well as gold and platinum records.

In a short time, Joe, Katherine, and the boys had traveled a long way from Gary, Indiana, to their luxury home in Encino, California.

"In Gary, we had two bedrooms, one for our parents and one for all of us. You *had* to be close. . . . But in Encino, the place was so big we had to make plans in advance to see each other. I think that Michael, in particular, was unhappy there. He felt, as I did, that we were all losing touch with each other."

—*Jermaine Jackson,* Michael Jackson: The Magic, The Madness, The Whole Story

Michael and Jermaine performing on a Bob Hope television special during the 1970s.

"Mama's Pearl" and "Never Can Say Goodbye"

- "Mama's Pearl," released in January 1971, peaked at No. 2 in the United States.

- The song, as written by Fonce Mizell and Freddie Perren, was originally called "Guess Who's Making Whoopie (with Your Girlfriend)." When producer Deke Richards heard 12-year-old Michael singing about girl swapping, he had them change the lyrics.

- "Never Can Say Goodbye" was released in March 1971 and also reached No. 2 on the Billboard Hot 100.

- Composed by Clifton Davis, this song would become one of the major hits of the disco era when recorded by Gloria Gaynor about three years later.

As evidenced in the photo above, Michael was growing fast by the time "Mama's Pearl" and "Never Can Say Goodbye" (opposite) were released in early 1971, but the songs' composers still had to write lyrics that were suitable for a 12-year-old to sing.

"One thing I have always told my boys is that you're either a winner in this life or a loser, and none of my kids were ever gonna be losers. I'm proud to say that they proved me right."

—Joseph Jackson, 1971

This promotional portrait of the Jackson family circa 1977 features everyone but Jermaine. Standing in back (left–right) is Jackie, Michael, Tito, and Marlon; in front (left–right) are Janet, Randy, LaToya, and Rebbie.

J5's Motown Singles

Year	Song	Peak Billboard Hot 100 Position
1969	"I Want You Back"	1
1970	"ABC"	1
1970	"The Love You Save"	1
1970	"I'll Be There"	1
1971	"Mama's Pearl"	2
1971	"Never Can Say Goodbye"	2
1971	"Maybe Tomorrow"	20
1971	"Sugar Daddy"	10
1972	"Little Bitty Pretty One"	13

Although "Never Can Say Good-bye" (left) climbed to No. 2 for The J5 in 1971, Gloria Gaynor's souped-up cover version just three years later helped to define the disco era. "The Love You Save" (right) was a monster hit, selling nearly two million copies.

Year	Song	Peak Billboard Hot 100 Position
1972	"Lookin' Through the Windows"	16
1972	"Corner of the Sky"	18
1973	"Hallelujah Day"	28
1973	"Get It Together"	28
1974	"Dancing Machine"	2
1974	"Whatever You Got I Want"	38
1974	"I Am Love"	15
1975	"Forever Came Today"	60

"I'll Be There" twice topped the Billboard Hot 100—first for The Jackson 5 in 1970 and then for Mariah Carey in 1992, when a single was created from her live performance of the song on MTV's Unplugged.

SPOTLIGHT ON

"Got to Be There"

In the summer of 1971, 13-year-old Donny Osmond branched out from singing with his brothers and achieved solo success with the single "Sweet and Innocent," which peaked at No. 7 in the United States. That September, he did even better when his cover of "Go Away, Little Girl" spent three weeks atop the Billboard Hot 100. That was all it took for Joseph Jackson and Berry Gordy to decide that "Got to Be There," originally intended for The Jackson 5, should instead be Michael's first solo release. Featuring backing vocals by Marlon and Jackie, this mid-tempo ballad served as the perfect showcase for the 13-year-old's remarkable voice. And by peaking at No. 4 in the United States and No. 5 in the United Kingdom, it served notice to his brothers and the world that MJ could have his own career.

opposite With its Top 5 chart success on both sides of the Atlantic, "Got to Be There" clearly showed that Michael could prosper as a solo artist.
right A portrait of MJ taken around the time of the record's release.

"I wanted more than anything to be a
typical little boy."
—Michael Jackson

Battle of the Half-Pints

One was black, the other was white, and color had an impact on mainstream acceptability during the early Seventies. Yet Michael Jackson and Donny Osmond also had a great deal in common. About nine months older than Michael, Osmond was the seventh of nine children, as was MJ. At the age of five, both joined a group that already comprised four older brothers. And both entered their teens as stars in their own right by augmenting group activities with successful solo pursuits. There, however, the similarities largely ended. While Michael was a pocket-sized prodigy, performing most of The J5's soul-based lead vocals and executing stunning dance moves, Osmond was part of a clean-cut vocal group that progressed from barbershop music to middle-of-the-road pop. And at a time when African Americans didn't make the covers of teen magazines nearly as often as their white counterparts, Osmond initially enjoyed even greater solo success than Michael. Within a few years, however, Michael would turn that situation on its head.

"It don't matter if you're black or white..." Although Donny Osmond enjoyed greater solo success than Michael during the early 1970s, MJ would soon reverse that trend in a way that neither young artist could ever have imagined.

"He'd call me up and say, 'You know, you're the only person in the world that I can talk to about certain things—about my childhood, my teen years—that can really understand.' Because we both lived it in a parallel universe."

—*Donny Osmond, 2009*

TV Specials

- On September 16, 1971, ABC aired The Jackson 5's first television special, Goin' Back to Indiana, *featuring the contributions of all nine siblings.*

- In addition to tracks recorded by The J5 during a May 29 homecoming concert in Gary, the show featured guest appearances by the likes of Diana Ross, Bobby Darin, Bill Cosby, and Tommy Smothers.

- The soundtrack album from the show sold just over 2.5 million copies worldwide.

- On November 5, 1972, ABC broadcast a second special, The Jackson 5 Show.

- This again featured the group members performing comedy skits, as well as songs such as "I Want You Back"; "Ben"; and a medley of "ABC," "I'll Be There," "The Love You Save," and "Never Can Say Goodbye."

In 1971 and 1972 The Jackson 5 continued to break racial barriers by hosting their own ABC TV specials. Bill Cosby joins the boys on the 1971 show (left), while Michael (opposite) is all smiles during the 1972 special.

"Rockin' Robin" and "Ben"

After recording a cover of Bobby Day's 1958 hit "Rockin' Robin" for his 1971 debut solo album, *Got to Be There*, Michael matched the Billboard Hot 100 position of Day's single when his own version peaked at No. 2 in February 1972. A few months later, MJ enjoyed his first solo chart topper... with a heartrending ballad about a psychic, psychotic rat that had originally been written for Donny Osmond. When Osmond turned down "Ben," Michael recorded the number

Early on, Michael's solo career was in the ascendancy, with the No. 2 success of "Rockin' Robin" being followed by his first chart topper, "Ben."

that he would later describe as one of his favorites, not least because it was the theme song to a horror movie of the same name. The song was nominated for an Academy Award in 1973 for Best Original Song, and Michael performed it at the televised ceremony that year.

Childhood Books

Peter Pan by James Matthew Barrie

Jonathan Livingston Seagull by Richard Bach

The Old Man and the Sea by Ernest Hemingway

Rip Van Winkle by Washington Irving

 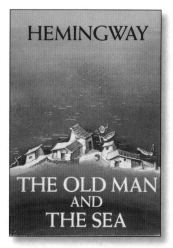

One of Michael's favorite pastimes throughout his life was reading. Peter Pan *by James Matthew Barrie (above left)* and Ernest Hemingway's The Old Man and the Sea *(above right)* were two cherished stories from MJ's childhood.

"It was sheer pandemonium. It was near chaos. It was frightening. It was JACKSONMANIA."

—*Motown press release, November 22, 1972, describing The Jackson 5's first European concert tour*

Going International

Fan hysteria surrounded The Jackson 5 when they toured Europe in November 1972, commencing with the Royal Variety Performance in front of Queen Elizabeth II.

Barely into his teens, Michael received fan mail by the sack load (left), while he and his brothers quickly grew accustomed to posing for photos with their devotees wherever they went (above).

MJ's Motown Singles

Year	Song	Peak Billboard Hot 100 Position
1971	"Got to Be There"	4
1972	"Rockin' Robin"	2
1972	"I Wanna Be Where You Are"	16
1972	"Ben"	1
1973	"With a Child's Heart"	50
1975	"Just a Little Bit of You"	23
1975	"We're Almost There"	54

"Rockin' Robin" reached No. 2 on the charts when performed by its original artist, Bobby Day, in 1958 and by Michael Jackson in 1972.

Up and Down the Charts

"Lookin' Through The Windows"

- In 1972, Michael won the first of his 40 Billboard Music Awards, topping the categories for Top Singles Artist of the Year and Top Male Singles Artist of the Year.

- That same year, MJ also received a Golden Globe for "Ben" as Best Original Song in a movie.

- Following these triumphs, Michael's solo success fizzled. Between 1973 and 1975, his three U.S. singles failed to reach the Top 20, while his two albums peaked at 92 and 101.

By the time Michael and his siblings released their seventh studio album, most of them were complaining about how Motown was handling their career. The only exception was Jermaine, who was about to become Berry Gordy's son-in-law.

- The Jackson 5 fared a little better, but they weren't able to repeat the chart achievements of their first six singles until 1974's "Dancing Machine."

Music & Me

When 14-year-old Michael recorded his third solo album in late 1972 and early 1973, his voice was in transition—and so were his musical aspirations. A couple of years earlier, Marvin Gaye had produced his classic album *What's Goin On*, and more recently Stevie Wonder had done the same on *Music of My Mind*. Michael considered it only natural for Motown to allow him a little more input on his own record, such as writing some of the songs. That didn't happen, however, and he also didn't play any instruments on the record, despite an album cover photo of him strumming an acoustic guitar. In the middle of a Jackson 5 world tour, MJ was unable to promote the album as much as it required. His cover of Wonder's "With a Child's Heart" barely scraped into the Top 50 on the Billboard Hot 100, and *Music & Me* climbed only as high as 92.

Despite a cover photo that depicted him as a budding guitar virtuoso, Michael didn't play any instruments on his third solo album.

Changing Vocal Style

- During his early years, Michael was a boy soprano.
- By 1975 he was a high tenor.
- The first time he employed his famous "vocal hiccup" was on 1973's "It's Too Late to Change the Time" from The J5 album G.I.T. Get It Together.
- His adult tenor and stunning falsetto were shown off to full effect on 1979's Off the Wall album.

Michael's voice changed significantly between 1971 and 1975—the years these two photos were taken.

MJ's Motown Albums

Year	Album	Peak Billboard 200 Position
1972	Got to Be There	14
1972	Ben	5
1973	Music & Me	92
1975	Forever, Michael	101

Although Michael's solo career got off to a flying start with his debut album Got to Be There, his success—and that of The Jackson 5—declined during the mid-1970s.

Taking on the World

Between March 1973 and February 1975, The Jackson 5's first world tour saw them perform concerts in Japan, Hawaii, the United Kingdom, South America, Hong Kong, Australia, New Zealand, the Philippines, and the West Indies.

left In May 1973, shortly after commencing their first world tour, The Jackson 5 appeared in Japan. *above* The final concerts took place in Britain in February 1975.

G.I.T. Get It Together

- *Released in September 1973, G.I.T. Get It Together was The Jackson 5's seventh studio album.*

- *The album signaled a change of musical direction from bubblegum to soul-based funk.*

- *This was the first album to feature all five of the brothers performing lead vocals, and Michael's voice had become noticeably deeper.*

- *Produced by Hal Davis and Norman Whitfield, the tracks on G.I.T. Get It Together flowed from one to the other, with no silence in between.*

above Michael's voice was noticeably different on G.I.T. Get It Together—even the high notes that only Michael could hit were retired. opposite MJ's looks continued to change as well, as seen in this shot circa 1974.

"When we started out, I used to be little, cute, and charming. Now I'm big, cute, and charming."

—*Michael Jackson, 1973*

Growing Pains

By 1973, things were changing for—and around—Michael and his siblings. At Motown, instead of just recording infectious pop songs whose appeal crossed over into the all-important white market, artists such as Marvin Gaye and Stevie Wonder were now immersing themselves in more socially conscious music lyrics that earned them even greater respect from black audiences. Furthermore, while Berry Gordy became increasingly involved with his company's expansion into film projects and pushing Diana Ross's movie career, he placed Ewart Abner in charge of record production. Soon the members of The Jackson 5 grew frustrated at the formulaic approach to their work and their lack of creative input.

By the time of their sixth studio album, the siblings were tired and frustrated with the music that Motown was forcing them to record. The gloomy expressions on the cover of Skywriter *only emphasized their dissatisfaction.*

"Dancing Machine"

The closing track on The Jackson 5's 1973 album, *G.I.T. Get It Together*, "Dancing Machine" became a smash hit after it was released in February 1974. Featuring lead vocals by Michael and Jermaine, sophisticated musicianship, synthesized effects, and backing vocals by six of the Jackson brothers (including 11-year-old Randy), the single sold more than three million copies and returned the group to the Top Ten for the first time since 1971, reaching No. 2 on the Billboard Hot 100. Michael was so enamored with the track's heavy funk groove that he was determined to find a new dance move to make it more exciting for people to watch and for him to perform. The result: MJ's popularizing of the "Robot."

After "Dancing Machine" returned The J5 to the upper reaches of the singles charts, the infectious track was included on their 1974 album of the same name.

The quintet showcasing their moves during a performance circa 1974.

"I never studied dancing before. It always came natural for me. Whenever I was little, any music would start, they couldn't sit me down. They couldn't *tie* me down, actually."

—Michael Jackson, on Jesse Jackson's Keep Hope Alive *radio program, 2005*

The Robot

- The Robot, also known as the Mannequin, replicates a robot's movements, including abrupt starts and stops that convey the idea of motorized, mechanical body parts.
- Similar dance moves were first seen among street performers, who mimed the motions of a mechanical man or puppet, without music.
- Charles Washington, a dancer on the TV program Soul Train, coupled his robotic moves with music to create the Robot in the late 1960s.
- Michael's first public performance of the Robot took place while he and his brothers performed "Dancing Machine" during the November 3, 1973, episode of Soul Train.
- After Michael's Soul Train performance helped propel "Dancing Machine" up the Billboard Hot 100, the Robot became a staple of his live act for the next few years.

Michael (in orange, second from right) leads the way, robot dancing onstage in Jamaica in early 1975.

Forever, Michael

The only Michael Jackson studio album to not take its name from one of its tracks, *Forever, Michael* was 16-year-old MJ's final solo outing before departing Motown. It was also an indication of the musical direction that he'd pursue on his records for Epic. Still, even though a smooth, contemporary soul sound was now part of his persona, it didn't help revive Michael's flagging fortunes on the charts. Recorded in 1974, the album was held back due to the success of "Dancing Machine" and finally released in January 1975. While the leadoff single "We're Almost There" climbed to No. 23 on the Billboard Hot 100, "Just a Little Bit of You" stalled at No. 54 and the album "peaked" at 101 on the Billboard 200. Nevertheless, in 1981 Motown capitalized on the success of MJ's 1979 Epic record *Off the Wall* by issuing "One Day in Your Life" as a single off *Forever, Michael*. That June the single spent two weeks at No. 1 in the United Kingdom.

"We're Almost There" and "Just a Little Bit of You,"
the two singles released off Forever, Michael in 1975, were written
by Eddie and Brian Holland, two-thirds of the legendary Motown
composing/production team of Holland-Dozier-Holland.

Bye-Bye, Berry

Fed up with not being allowed to contribute their own compositions or play their own instruments in the studio, The Jackson 5 left Motown after the May 1975 release of their ninth studio album, *Moving Violation*. They also left behind the group's name and several of its members. The most notable among these was Jermaine, who had married Berry Gordy's daughter Hazel and opted to remain with his father-in-law to pursue a solo career, much to the hurt and anger of Joseph Jackson. (The other departees were drummer Johnny Jackson and keyboard player Ronnie Rancifer.) Then, when Joe negotiated a better deal with CBS, Gordy retaliated by pointing out that the group could no longer use The Jackson 5 name, which was owned by Motown. Thereafter, 13-year-old Randy replaced Jermaine, and at Michael's suggestion he and his brothers became simply The Jacksons.

"The Jackson 5 is a family affair, and we plan to keep it that way.... We will be making some individual recordings, but we would strongly resist any efforts to break us up as a group."

—Michael Jackson

All smiles in front of The J5 logo that, along with the Jackson 5 name, was retained by Motown after the group's acrimonious split with the label.

Chapter 3

"Don't Stop 'til You Get Enough"— Ascending to the Moonwalk

"He *raised the bar* and then broke the bar. His talent and creativity thrust him and entertainment into *another* stratosphere."

—Berry Gordy, at MJ's memorial service, July 7, 2009

Michael Jackson in 1983, posing in the zippered red leather jacket that would become symbolic of the Thriller era.

New Label, New Contract

- The Jacksons' new contract with CBS provided the group with a royalty rate of 27 percent per record instead of the 2.7 percent that they had been paid by Motown.

- The first two albums under the new label were produced by the Philadelphia International team of Kenny Gamble and Leon Huff, architects of the soul-based "Philly Sound" that rivaled Motown's and produced hits by artists such as The O'Jays.

- Because Berry Gordy refused the Recording Industry Association of America access to Motown's accounts, The Jacksons, released in November 1976, was the group's first gold album. It included the Gamble/Huff hit single "Enjoy Yourself"; Michael's first solo composition, "Blues Away"; and a number MJ wrote with Tito called "Style of Life."

- Goin' Places, released in October 1977, was one of the worst-selling albums by The Jacksons, but the group-penned club hit "Different Kind of Lady" did inspire the brothers to produce and write all of the songs for their next record.

The renamed and reformatted first two albums by The Jacksons for CBS Records' Philadelphia International label provided the group with a more contemporary sound and greater artistic control. However, they didn't signal an upswing in the group's chart fortunes.

The Jacksons

When asked to host a CBS television variety show with his siblings (including sisters Rebbie, LaToya, and Janet), Michael had some serious reservations. Never mind that *The Jacksons* was the first variety show to be hosted by an African American family, as well as the first in which the entire cast was related; none of them were Ed Sullivan, and Michael knew it. Yet, when he warned Joe and other family members that such a move would hurt record sales, they disagreed. Michael was forced to join in all the "fun" between June 1976 and March 1977, participating in comedy skits, performing hastily choreographed dance routines, and introducing guest stars ranging from Redd Foxx and Muhammad Ali to Sonny Bono and David Letterman. As it happens, the show was a hit, and the network wanted a second season. Michael refused, and nobody could argue—record sales had indeed been hurt, and both the group's albums and singles had dropped on the charts between 1976 and 1977.

Despite the smiles, Michael wasn't happy about hosting a TV variety show with his siblings, seen here during a taping at CBS's Burbank Studios in November 1976. Pictured left to right are Randy, LaToya, Marlon, Janet, MJ, Jackie, Rebbie, and Tito.

The Jacksons on the Charts (1976–1984)

SINGLES

Year	Song	Peak Billboard Hot 100 Position
1976	"Enjoy Yourself"	6
1977	"Show You the Way to Go"	28
1977	"Goin' Places"	52
1978	"Blame It on the Boogie"	54
1979	"Shake Your Body (Down to the Ground)"	7
1980	"Lovely One"	12

Although "Show You the Way to Go" (near right) and "Blame It on the Boogie" (opposite, right) were chart hits in the UK, The Jacksons didn't enjoy similar success in the United States until the release of "Shake Your Body (Down to the Ground)" (opposite, left).

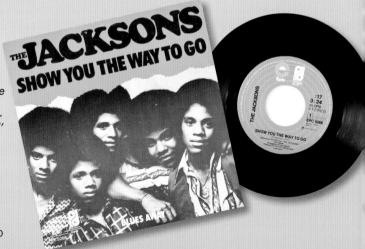

Year	Song	Peak Billboard Hot 100 Position
1980	"This Place Hotel"	22
1981	"Can You Feel It"	77
1981	"Walk Right Now"	73
1984	"State of Shock" (with Mick Jagger)	3
1984	"Torture"	17
1984	"Body"	47

"Don't Stop 'til You Get Enough" ♕ 133

Destiny

■ Released on the CBS label Epic Records in December 1978, this was the first album by The Jacksons to be produced by the brothers and contain their own compositions.

■ The siblings composed most of the material in the studio at their home on Hayvenhurst Avenue in Encino and recorded it within a couple of months.

■ Peaking at No. 11 on the Billboard 200 chart, Destiny reestablished The Jacksons as a hit group.

■ Destiny was the group's first album to be certified platinum for sales of more than one million copies.

■ Two songs from Destiny were released as singles in the United States. The first, "Blame It on the Boogie," didn't crack the Top 50, but the second, "Shake Your Body (Down to the Ground)," reached No. 7 on the Billboard Hot 100 and was one of the main reasons for the album's overall success.

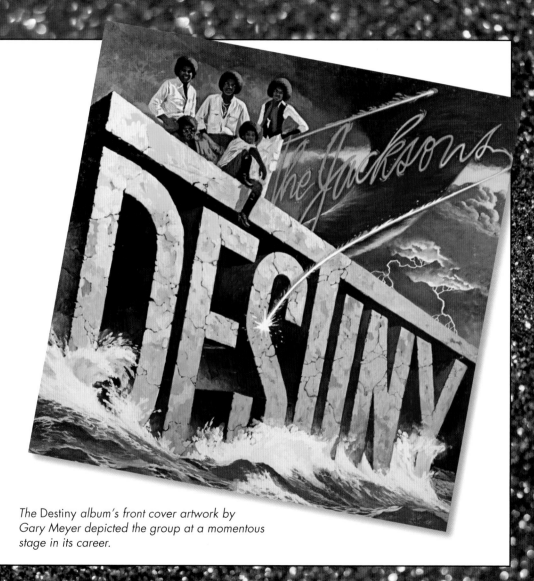

The Destiny album's front cover artwork by Gary Meyer depicted the group at a momentous stage in its career.

"Michael is like the golden watch that
makes everything tick."

—Joseph Jackson, Vibe, February 1979

MJ during a performance with The Jacksons at
Rhode Island's Nassau Coliseum in 1979.

"Shake Your Body (Down to the Ground)"

Originally titled "Shake a Body" when written by Michael and Randy, "Shake Your Body (Down to the Ground)" made the Top Ten on the Billboard Hot 100 and achieved double-platinum status following its release on December 9, 1978. Interestingly enough, there was a world of difference between the three-minute, 54-second edit issued to radio stations; the eight-minute version that appeared on the *Destiny* album; and the 12-inch's extended eight-minute, 37-second disco remix that was played in the clubs. For one thing, the 12-inch featured an ascending three-octave vocal part that didn't appear on the other versions. Still, aside from returning The Jacksons to the upper echelons of the singles charts, the song is notable for becoming the last one the group ever performed live together when they sang it during the Michael Jackson: 30th Anniversary Concert at New York's Madison Square Garden on September 10, 2001—the night before the 9/11 attacks.

In the more than 20 years between the release of "Shake Your Body (Down to the Ground)" and that track serving as The Jacksons' swan song during Michael's 30th anniversary concert (pictured), he and his brothers underwent many changes in appearance, as well as in their personal and professional fortunes.

Battle of the Boogie

Despite working with artists such as David Knopfler, Eric Burdon, and Barry Manilow, English singer-songwriter Mick Jackson is best known for "Blame It on the Boogie." In 2010 he was the subject of the British TV documentary The Other Michael Jackson: Battle of the Boogie.

"Blame It on the Boogie," the only track on the *Destiny* album not written by Michael, Jackie, Randy, or any of the brothers, was still credited to a couple of Jacksons—English singer-songwriter Mick Jackson and his brother David—as well as to musician Elmar Krohn. And although a peak chart position of 54 wasn't enough to ensure success in the United States, it was a different story in the United Kingdom, where the single competed against the version issued on Atlantic by Mick in what the press dubbed a "Battle of the Boogie." Released in October 1978, the two "Boogies" shared media attention as well as sales, with Mick performing his song on the highly rated BBC television show *Top of the Pops* a week before The Jacksons. However, it was the American group's version that won out, climbing to No. 8 on the UK chart during the first week of November after the recording by "the other Michael Jackson" peaked at No. 15.

The Jacksons on the Charts (1976–1984)

ALBUMS

Year	Album	Peak Billboard 200 Position
1976	*The Jacksons*	36
1977	*Goin' Places*	63
1978	*Destiny*	11
1980	*Triumph*	10
1984	*Victory*	4

It was largely thanks to the hit single "Shake Your Body (Down to the Ground)" that the Destiny album became a chart success.

SPOTLIGHT ON

The Wiz

Some projects look like they can't fail. So imagine the excitement when, in 1977, Motown Productions acquired the film rights to *The Wiz*, an all-black Broadway musical adaptation of L. Frank Baum's *The Wonderful Wizard of Oz* that had recently won seven Tony Awards. Diana Ross was cast as a grown-up Dorothy in modern-day Manhattan alongside Michael Jackson as the Scarecrow, Richard Pryor as the Wiz, and Lena Horne as Glinda the Good Witch. Having initially refused 33-year-old Ross's request to play 24-year-old Dorothy, Berry Gordy acquiesced when Universal agreed to fund the project if she was the star. With seasoned director Sidney Lumet at the helm and Quincy Jones supervising the music, a box-office hit seemed certain.

Filmed in late 1977 at Astoria Studios in Queens, New York, and at a variety of other NYC locations, *The Wiz* was the most expensive movie shot in the Big Apple up to that time. Unfortunately, in return for its $24 million budget, it only grossed around $13 million following its October 1978 release in the United States. Critics saved most of their kinder comments for MJ's big-screen debut and his performance of "You Can't Win, You Can't Break Even," which had him crooning with a quartet of crows, and "Ease On Down the Road," which he sang with Ross and other cast members as they danced down the Yellow Brick Road. In addition to being used as the film's theme, the latter was released as a single, peaking at No. 41 on the

While Dorothy, the Scarecrow, the Tin Man, and the Cowardly Lion danced their way through Manhattan in The Wiz, *the only character who didn't really change from* The Wizard of Oz *was Dorothy's cairn terrier, Toto.*

Billboard Hot 100. Still, Michael—who had unintentionally antagonized Ross by learning the dance routines far more quickly than she did—loved the entire moviemaking experience, which endowed him with greater confidence about his talents.

"It's good that the Scarecrow is the first traveling companion [Dorothy] meets; Michael Jackson fills the role with humor and warmth."

—*Roger Ebert, in his* Chicago Sun-Times *review of* The Wiz, *October 24, 1978*

The star-studded cast of The Wiz *(left–right): Michael Jackson, Nipsey Russell, Diana Ross, and Ted Ross.*

MJ'S FIRSTS

Group single: "Big Boy" (1968)

No. 1 group single: "I Want You Back" (1969)

Group album: *Diana Ross Presents The Jackson 5* (1969)

Solo single: "Got to Be There" (1971)

No. 1 solo single: "Ben" (1972)

Solo album: *Got to Be There* (1972)

Movie: *The Wiz* (1978)

Solo tour: 1987 *Bad* World Tour

From "Big Boy" (above), The J5's debut single on Steeltown Records, through "Ben," Michael's earliest chart topper, on through his initial solo tour (right), the firsts in MJ's career increased in reach, but all were critical to his growth as an artist.

Quincy Jones

Conductor, arranger, producer, composer, trumpeter—Quincy Delight Jones Jr. has been all of these and more during a long music career that has earned him a record

79 Grammy nominations and 27 Grammy Awards, including one for Grammy Legend in 1991. By then, his work with artists such as Frank Sinatra, Ella Fitzgerald, Peggy Lee, Count Basie, Duke Ellington, and Dinah Washington, as well as his work on the soundtracks of more than 30 major movies, had already been superseded by his achievements with Michael Jackson. After befriending MJ on the movie set of *The Wiz*, Jones received a call from the young entertainer, asking him to recommend someone who could produce his next solo album. Jones halfheartedly suggested a few names, then asked, "Why don't you let *me* do it?" So began a collaboration that saw an introverted Michael transform into the confident, assertive artist whose landmark 1979 album, *Off the Wall*, benefited from the producer's belief in his talents and the creative freedom to perform some of his own material.

Having worked with such luminaries as Frank Sinatra (above, right), *Quincy Jones* (opposite and above, left) *was already an accomplished musician, songwriter, arranger, and producer when he first encountered Michael Jackson. Nevertheless, their collaboration on* Off the Wall *catapulted Q's career to another level.*

Off the Wall

Following a string of so-so solo albums that had curbed Michael's creative freedom and only hinted at his musical talents, *Off the Wall* allowed him to fully express his tastes for funk, soul, disco, jazz, and pop while displaying the exceptional vocal and compositional abilities that would soon transport him to even greater heights. Recorded between December 1978 and June 1979, the album had a smoother, more sophisticated soul-pop sound than that found on The Jacksons records, and it was the first by a solo artist to spawn four Top Ten U.S. singles: "Don't Stop 'til You Get Enough" (which Michael wrote), "Rock with You," the title track, and "She's Out of My Life." Critics fell over themselves in their praise following its August 1979 release. *Rolling Stone* compared MJ's "extraordinarily beautiful" singing to that of Stevie Wonder, while music critic Robert Christgau described the album as "the dance groove of the year."

Although *Off the Wall* sold more than 20 million copies worldwide and laid the groundwork for Michael's next and biggest success, he was upset that the album only won a single Grammy Award, receiving Best Male R&B Vocal Performance for "Don't Stop 'til You Get Enough." That track won him three American Music Awards, and MJ also received Billboard Music Awards for Top Black Artist and Top Black Album. Despite these honors, Michael felt that, when it came to the Grammys, he had basically been rejected by his peers. "That experience lit a fire in my soul," he'd later recall in *Moon Walk*. "All I could think of was the next album and what I would do with it. I wanted it to be truly great."

While Off the Wall*'s front cover shot of a tuxedoed Michael Jackson gave no clue as to how much his appearance would soon change, the glowing socks on the back cover did presage his iconic image.*

"Off the Wall

represents discofied

post-Motown glamour

at its classiest."

—Rolling Stone,
November 1, 1979

*Michael showing
off his moves—and
plenty of sequins—
during the Destiny
tour in 1979.*

JUST the Facts

Off the Wall Contributors

- *Several songwriters contributed to Off the Wall, including Paul McCartney and Stevie Wonder.*

- *The album was originally titled Girlfriend, after McCartney had written a song by that name for Michael and recorded it for his 1978 album London Town. MJ's version was released as a single only in the UK.*

Among the major talents who contributed to Off the Wall was Paul McCartney, with whom Michael enjoyed a solid friendship for several years.

- *Michael was so moved by "She's Out of My Life," a song written by Tom Bahler about the end of his relationship with Karen Carpenter, that he kept getting choked up at the end of each take—which can be heard on the finished record.*

- *"I Can't Help It"—cowritten by Stevie Wonder with Susaye Greene— was the closest MJ ever came to performing a pure jazz song on any of his records.*

John Branca

In 1979, at the age of 21 and after the huge success of *Off the Wall*, Michael felt it was time to exercise greater control over his career. He decided to hire his own entertainment lawyer, 31-year-old John Branca, and told the young attorney to make him the biggest, wealthiest star in show business. Branca, who has represented artists such as The Rolling Stones, Bob Dylan, The Bee Gees, The Beach Boys, Don Henley, ZZ Top, Fleetwood Mac, and Neil Diamond, renegotiated Michael's

existing deals so that he earned a far higher royalty from CBS Records and could quit The Jacksons whenever he wanted. Branca subsequently confirmed his worth by attaining financing of more than a million dollars to produce the "Thriller" video and by brokering the purchase of ATV Music, which included The Beatles song catalog. Having parted ways with MJ between 1990 and 1993, as well as between 2006 and 2009, Branca was rehired just three weeks before Michael's death.

Entertainment lawyer John Branca played a huge role in helping Michael Jackson to become the biggest star of the 1980s.

Food

Vegetarian

Mexican

Fish and sushi

Fresh fruit

Pizza

Popcorn

Glazed doughnuts

Sunflower seeds

Frosted Flakes

M&Ms

Triumph

In July 1980 The Jacksons released *Triumph,* their 13th studio album. It featured material composed by Michael, Jackie, Randy, and Tito, as well as bass player Mike McKinney, who, along with guitarist David Williams, was now a member of the touring band. While producing the record themselves, the brothers shared the vocal chores, with Michael still handling most of the leads. The result was a platinum album that peaked at No. 10 in the United States and sold more than two million copies worldwide. Okay, so it was no *Off the Wall,* but it did produce three singles: "Lovely One," which hit No. 12 in the United States; "Heartbreak Hotel," which reached 22 before having its name changed to "This Place Hotel" in 1984 so it wouldn't clash with Elvis Presley's 1956 hit; and "Can You Feel It," which climbed to No. 77 in the United States and No. 6 in the United Kingdom.

Released in the summer of 1980, and benefiting from Michael's recent solo success, Triumph *(opposite) was the Jackson brothers' first Top Ten album since 1972's* Lookin' Through the Windows *and provided the group with solid material for an accompanying concert tour (above).*

"Michael is very **happy** when he's **onstage**. Every night before the show, he's the first one dressed and **ready to go**."

—*Frank DiLeo, Life, September 1984*

Michael in his comfort zone, onstage at The Forum in Los Angeles in 1981.

Triumph Tour

- ■ Running from July 8 to September 26, 1981, the Triumph U.S. concert tour comprised 39 shows in 33 cities.

- ■ Michael was involved in the design of the Close Encounters of the Third Kind–inspired stage set.

- ■ Magician Doug Henning helped create the special effects, including MJ disappearing in a puff of smoke at the end of "Don't Stop 'til You Get Enough."

- ■ The Triumph tour grossed $5.5 million and featured songs from The Jacksons' Epic catalog, a medley of its Motown hits, and five numbers from Michael's Off the Wall album.

Not only was Michael the main attraction of The Jacksons' 1981 Triumph tour, but he also contributed to the set and costume design and the choreography.

"I lived in an area called Encino, and I used to see signs of graffiti saying 'Disco Sucks' and 'Disco is this' and 'Disco is that.' Disco was just a happy medium of making people dance at the time, but it was so popular that society was turning against it. I said, I'm just going to do a great album . . . an album where every song is like a hit record."

—Michael Jackson, on Jesse Jackson's Keep Hope Alive radio show, 2005

opposite The King of Pop with the Queen of Disco: During the late 1970s and early 1980s, Michael Jackson and Donna Summer were two of the world's hottest stars. In 1982 Michael provided backing vocals on Summer's self-titled album, produced by Quincy Jones. left This sticker represents the feelings of many music lovers during the 1970s.

SPOTLIGHT ON

Thriller

It was—and still is—the bestselling album of all time, spending 37 weeks atop the Billboard 200 chart (out of its 80 consecutive weeks in the Top Ten), scooping a record-breaking eight Grammy Awards, and initially shifting around 40 million copies worldwide (a figure that, according to current estimates, has since swelled to as many as 110 million copies). If Michael Jackson was determined to outstrip the suc-

Portrait artist Dick Zimmerman shot the cover photos for Thriller *and, when Michael couldn't find a suitable costume to wear, lent him his white suit.*

cess of *Off the Wall* and earn the undying respect of fans, critics, and fellow musicians, he surpassed even his own wildest dreams with *Thriller*. The album was the first LP to deliver seven Top Ten singles in the United States: "The Girl Is Mine" (with Paul McCartney), "Billie Jean," "Beat It," "Wanna Be Startin' Somethin'," "Human Nature," "P.Y.T. (Pretty Young Thing)," and the title track.

Between April and November 1982, working with a then-massive $750,000 budget, Michael and coproducer Quincy Jones ran through an estimated 300 songs before completing the nine tracks that ended up on the record. Four of these—"Wanna Be Startin' Somethin'," "The Girl Is Mine," "Beat It," and "Billie Jean"—were written by MJ, and the result was something for everyone: hard funk, smooth soul, tender ballads, classic disco, and even cutting-edge rock—as displayed by Eddie Van Halen's guitar solo on "Beat It." The album's success was enhanced by groundbreaking videos that made Michael an MTV phenomenon and established black music as part of the mainstream. Just as Elvis Presley and The Beatles are synonymous with the music of the 1950s and '60s, Michael Jackson was the pop superstar of the 1980s, and many critics were quick to confirm this. "In the world of pop music, there is Michael Jackson and there is everybody else," asserted the *New York Times*, while *Time* magazine described MJ as "a one-man rescue team for the music business. A songwriter who sets the beat for a decade. A dancer with the fanciest feet on the street. A singer who cuts across all boundaries of taste and style, and color too."

"Michael sang his booty off. We'd stay up five days with no sleep because we were so excited."

—*Quincy Jones, on recording the* Thriller *album*

MJ, his eight Grammys, and Quincy Jones in 1984.

BY THE NUMBERS

MJ on the Charts (1979–1984)

Year	Song	Peak Billboard Hot 100 Position
1979	"Don't Stop 'til You Get Enough"	1
1979	"Rock with You"	1
1979	"Off the Wall"	10
1980	"She's Out of My Life"	10
1981	"One Day in Your Life"	55
1982	"The Girl Is Mine" (with Paul McCartney)	2
1983	"Billie Jean"	1
1983	"Beat It"	1
1983	"Wanna Be Startin' Somethin'"	5
1983	"Human Nature"	7
1983	"P.Y.T. (Pretty Young Thing)"	10
1984	"Thriller"	4
1984	"Farewell My Summer Love"	38

About Face

While trying to execute a complex dance move in 1979, Michael tripped onstage and broke his nose. The resulting rhinoplasty was evident in the *Off the Wall* cover photo, which unveiled a smaller nose; breathing problems then led to a second surgery. Weight loss due to a macrobiotic diet—as well as soft curls in place of his Afro hairdo—added to the drastic change in Michael's appearance that was evident by the time of *Thriller*'s release.

Before and after: The late 1970s Michael Jackson looked considerably different than the early '80s version.

"Billie Jean"

"Billie Jean" and "Beat It" were Thriller's two No. 1 singles.

- Quincy Jones initially didn't consider "Billie Jean" a strong enough song to be included on the Thriller album. He also suggested that it be retitled "Not My Lover" to prevent people from mistakenly assuming the single was about tennis legend Billie Jean King.

- One of the top-selling singles of 1983, "Billie Jean" simultaneously topped the American and British charts before earning two Grammys among numerous music industry awards.

- The unusually dark-themed pop song was promoted by an equally groundbreaking video that depicted MJ making his way to a woman's bedroom while being pursued by a press photographer.

- The video was the first by a black artist to be aired regularly on the two-year-old MTV cable network. Consequently, it played a vital role in establishing the music channel, breaking down racial barriers, and sending sales of Thriller through the roof.

THE REAL BILLIE JEAN

While many listeners were under the false impression that Michael wrote "Billie Jean" about tennis superstar Billie Jean King, his biographer J. Randy Taraborrelli stated that the lyrics focused on a young female fan who stalked Michael and claimed he was the father of her baby. According to Taraborrelli, the woman wrote so many letters to MJ about "their" child—while enclosing photos of herself and the infant—that he had nightmares about her showing up at his home. His paranoia increased when she sent him a package that contained a weapon and a note instructing Michael to kill himself after she had shot herself and the baby. The woman was ultimately committed to a mental hospital. In his autobiography Michael asserted that Billie Jean was a composite of the people who had accused him and his brothers of fathering their children over the years.

So, who was "Billie Jean" really about?

"I've been told over and over again that black people on the covers of magazines don't sell copies. Just wait. Someday those magazines are going to be *begging* me for an interview. Maybe I'll give them one. And maybe I won't."

—*Michael Jackson, 1979*

It was hardly surprising to find The Jacksons on the cover of Ebony *or* Jet, *but for Michael to appear on such magazines as* Time *and* Life *was something that only he could have predicted.*

"Beat It"

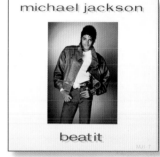

michael jackson

beat it

- Released on February 14, 1983, as Thriller's *third single, "Beat It" scooped the Grammy Awards for Record of the Year and Best Rock Vocal Performance.*

- *Michael wrote "Beat It" as a rock song aimed at school kids, with lyrics that urged them to try settling their differences without fighting.*

- *The promotional video, directed by Bob Giraldi and inspired by the musical* West Side Story, *depicts MJ breaking up a knife fight between two gang leaders and persuading their followers to join his dance routine.*

- *In addition to its 18 professional dancers, the video employed about 80 real-life gang members (to enhance its authenticity) and was choreographed by Michael Peters.*

While "Beat It" earned MJ Grammy Awards for his vocal performance and Record of the Year, the video highlighted his already well-known talents as a dancer.

Collaborations
(1978–1984)

"Ease on Down the Road" with Diana Ross (1978)

"Save Me" with Dave Mason (1980)

"Muscles" with Diana Ross (1982)

"Say Say Say" with Paul McCartney (1983)

"Somebody's Watching Me" with Rockwell and Jermaine Jackson (1984)

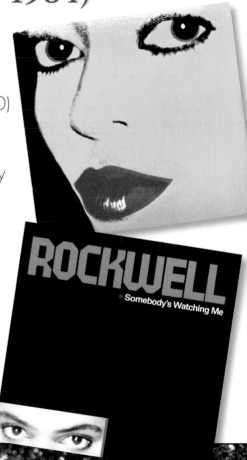

The eyes have it: While many people believed cosmetic surgery made Michael's peepers look similar to those of Diana Ross, Rockwell (Berry Gordy's son) is the one staring out from the sleeve of the single "Somebody's Watching Me."

"I love great music—it has no color, it has no boundaries."

—Michael Jackson, Vibe, March 2002

Michael's own great music broke down barriers between races, as performed here during a tour date in Kansas.

"Thriller" Video and Documentary

The "most famous music video of all time." That's how the 14-minute mini epic that Michael Jackson filmed to promote the song "Thriller" was described in December 2009, after it had become the first-ever pop video to be inducted into the National Film Registry of the Library of Congress. And with good reason. A parody of 1950s horror flicks, the "Thriller" video depicts MJ freaking out his girlfriend by turning into a werecat (the feline version of a werewolf) and dancing with a group of zombies. It was played in heavy rotation on MTV following its December 1983 release and elevated the art form to new heights courtesy of its choreography, special effects, and first-rate production values (all of which cost a then-record $1 million at a time when the average music video budget was about $50,000).

It was after Michael had seen Jon Landis's comic horror movie *An American Werewolf in London* that he asked the director to transform him into one of the undead. Jackson and Landis cowrote the

"Thriller" screenplay and recruited Rick Baker, who had created the special makeup effects for *An American Werewolf in London,* to do the same for "Thriller." Michael Peters took charge of the dance moves; former *Playboy* centerfold Ola Ray portrayed MJ's panic-stricken girlfriend; and, as on the record, horror movie legend Vincent Price contributed

Michael hung out with an eclectic assortment of characters through the years, but none were quite as strange or disturbing as his dancing partners in the "Thriller" video.

a characteristically spooky spoken-word performance. A one-hour documentary, *The Making of "Thriller,"* more than helped fund the enterprise, earning $250,000 from Showtime for ten days of exclusive broadcast rights, another $250,000 from MTV for two weeks of exclusive broadcast rights, and a whole lot more from Vestron Video for the sale of a record-breaking nine million copies on VHS. The net effect was even more widespread interest in black music, as well as a major shot in the arm for the pop industry and MTV.

Poetry in motion—Michael's smooth execution of his most famous dance move stunned fans, many of whom could hardly believe anyone could glide so effortlessly across a stage.

"From just riding through Harlem, I remember in the...late 70s, early 80s, I would see these kids dancing on the street and I would see these kids doing these, uh, sliding backwards, kinda like an 'illusion dancing' I call it.

I took a mental picture of it. A mental movie of it. I went

into my room upstairs in Encino, and I would just start

doing the dance, and create and perfect it. But, it

definitely started within the black culture."

—*Michael Jackson, on Jesse Jackson's* Keep Hope Alive *radio show, 2005*

Motown 25: Yesterday, Today, Forever

Never mind that Motown was founded in January 1959—evidently, no one could wait until January 1984 to celebrate the label's 25th anniversary. So, on March 25, 1983, a star-studded TV special was taped before a live audience; the celebration was then broadcast by NBC on May 16. Featuring appearances by such Motown luminaries as Mary Wells, Martha Reeves, and Stevie Wonder, the show also boasted Marvin Gaye's last TV appearance before his murder the following year; a "Battle of the Bands" between The Temptations and The Four Tops; and the reunions of Smokey Robinson and the Miracles, Diana Ross and the Supremes, and The Jackson 5. The J5 reunion featured Jermaine's first performance in eight years with Michael, Jackie, Marlon, and Tito, who were subsequently joined by Randy.

The highlight of the show—and, arguably, of Michael Jackson's career—took place after an emotional rendition of "I'll Be There," when his brothers left him alone onstage to sing his latest hit, "Billie

The emotional highlight of Motown's 25th anniversary special was Michael's duet with Jermaine on "I'll Be There."

Jean." Wearing the outfit that would thereafter comprise the iconic MJ image—black sequined jacket; silver sequined shirt; short black pants revealing white glitter socks; and a white, rhinestone-covered, left-hand glove—Michael executed the dance moves of James Brown, Sammy Davis Jr., Jackie Wilson, and Fred Astaire with breathtaking skill and agility. It was as if he was pulling out every trick in the book while performing his own trademark spins and unveiling the "moonwalk" that saw him glide smoothly in reverse. Michael's adaptation of the "locking" moves that he had seen on the streets of New York as well as on TV's *Soul Train*, the moonwalk stunned millions of viewers and served as the apotheosis of a performance that was, in a word, unforgettable.

Motown 25: Yesterday, Today, Forever *captured Michael Jackson at the peak of his career, turning in an unforgettable performance that would become part of his legacy.*

"Man, you really put them on their asses last night. You're an angry dancer. I'm the same way."

—Fred Astaire to Michael Jackson
after his Motown 25 performance

MJ, the Icon

black sequined jacket

white, rhinestone-covered, left-hand glove

silver sequined shirt

short black pants

white glitter socks

The black sequined jacket; the silver sequined shirt; the black pants that were short enough to reveal the white glitter socks; and, of course, the white, rhinestone-covered, left-hand glove—Michael's classic image was on full display that night.

Chapter 4

"Man in the Mirror"—
Changing Face, Changing Fortunes

"I do want to be perfect. *I look in the mirror, and I just* want to change, *and be better."*

—Michael Jackson

At the height of his popularity, Michael wows fans during a March 1988 installment of his Bad world tour at New York's Madison Square Garden.

The Pepsi Disaster

The date: Friday, January 27, 1984. The place: Shrine Auditorium in Los Angeles. The event: The filming of a Pepsi-Cola commercial featuring The Jacksons performing "You're a Whole New Generation," a specially rewritten version of "Billie Jean," before an audience of 3,000. While his brothers played the song onstage, Michael was to appear in silhouette and then descend a ramp with magnesium flash bombs exploding all around him. The problem was, contrary to safety regulations, two of the bombs were only a couple of feet from either side of MJ's head. During one of several takes, the sparks from the flash bombs set his hair on fire. Initially unaware, Michael danced down the ramp and performed some of his trademark spins. Then, overwhelmed by the flames, he fell to the ground and managed to extinguish them himself. Still, the damage had been done.

Meanwhile, Jermaine thought his brother had been shot, and stunned fans in the audience screamed. The crew rushed to Michael's aid, and he was sped by ambulance to the emergency room at Cedars-Sinai Medical Center. While in the hospital Michael reluctantly accepted a painkiller—the first of many that he would take over the years to combat the pain caused by second- and third-degree burns to the back of his head.

Panicking Pepsi executives contemplated the inevitable lawsuit and bad publicity—talk about achieving the exact opposite of what they had intended. MJ was subsequently treated at Brotman Memorial Hospital in Culver City, and he donated the $1.5 million settlement he received from Pepsi-Cola to the Michael Jackson Burn Center that was established there in his honor. He was fortunate to be alive . . . and Pepsi was lucky that the incident only served to publicize its commercial and increase the sales of its drink.

While Jermaine (left) is still unaware of the drama unfolding behind him, MJ's hair is ablaze during the taping of the infamous Pepsi TV commercial.

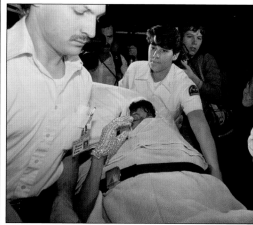

Michael still managed a wave for his fans while being wheeled into the hospital after the accident.

The King of Pop Meets the President

- On May 14, 1984, Michael visited the White House to accept an award from President Ronald Reagan for the pop star's support of charities that helped people deal with alcohol and drug problems.

- The visit was arranged by Transportation Secretary Elizabeth Dole in conjunction with Michael allowing his song "Beat It" to be used in television and radio campaigns against drunk driving.

- While the president and First Lady both wore smart suits, Michael's blue-sequined outfit and white rhinestone glove easily outsparkled his hosts.

- After the president presented Michael with the award, MJ and his entourage were given a tour of the White House and had a meeting with the Reagans and members of their staff.

"Well, isn't this a thriller?" President Ronald Reagan said, as he commenced his South Lawn speech to welcome Michael to the White House. The U.S. leader continued with the song references throughout the speech by saying his own remarks were "a little off the wall"; the Washington, D.C., fans "want you back"; and that, faced with the problem of drunk driving, the nation could "beat it."

Frank DiLeo

In early 1984, Michael was looking for a new manager. Since 1977 Papa Joe had been assisted by the team of Ron Weisner and Freddy DeMann, but their contract had expired and MJ was no longer enamored with the idea of having his father run his career. Accordingly, he interviewed several potential replacements, including Colonel Tom Parker, the man who had taken Elvis Presley from rags to riches. Michael settled upon what many industry observers thought was a surprising choice: Frank DiLeo. A native of Pittsburgh,

DiLeo started out as a record promoter's assistant before becoming national director of promotions for RCA Records. While serving as Epic's vice president of promotions, DiLeo impressed Michael with his contribution to the *Thriller* album's stunning success. What's more, the pop star admired DiLeo's self-confidence and outgoing personality—character traits that Michael himself didn't possess. DiLeo was just 36 when he became Michael Jackson's exclusive manager, having agreed that he wouldn't manage anyone else.

When Frank DiLeo attended the L.A. premiere of MJ's movie This Is It in October 2009 (opposite), it was amid much sadder circumstances than when he and Michael had arrived at London's Heathrow Airport during the *Bad* world tour just more than 20 years earlier (left).

The Jacksons' *Victory* Album and North American Tour

- *Released on July 6, 1984, the first day of the tour, Victory was The Jacksons' only studio collection to include all six brothers and the last one to feature Michael as a group member.*

- *The Grammy-nominated album peaked at No. 4 on the Billboard 200 and was certified double platinum while selling more than seven million copies worldwide.*

- *The tour, which ran until December 9, 1984, was sponsored by the Pepsi-Cola Company, promoted by boxing supremo Don King, and grossed a then-record $175 million.*

- *Since Michael refused to perform songs from the new album, the tour went ahead with a set list that featured numbers from Destiny and Triumph, as well as from Michael's and Jermaine's solo careers.*

- *Eddie Van Halen performed his "Beat It" guitar solo during the brothers' concert in Dallas.*

- *Michael wanted the tour to be titled "The Final Curtain," but he was outvoted by his brothers.*

Michael's outfits on the Victory tour were designed by Bill Whitten, the man who created his sequined glove along with numerous clothes for both MJ and The J5 over the years.

"This is our **last** and **final** show. It's been a long 20 years, and we love you all."

—Michael Jackson, while performing "Shake Your Body (Down to the Ground)" during The Jacksons' December 9, 1984, concert at L.A.'s Dodger Stadium

Victory Tour
Ticket Controversy

Michael had warned his five brothers not to do it—not to have Don King, a boxing promoter with a shady reputation, take charge of their 1984 *Victory* concert tour of North America. However, King's parallel reputation for earning megabucks had persuaded the group to outvote MJ on the matter. Michael had also advised The Jacksons to veto the ticket-distribution plan devised by King, Joe Jackson (who was still the group's manager), and tour organizer Chuck Sullivan. Again, no one listened. Tickets for the 55-concert stadium tour went on sale that June, with applicants obliged to send a money order of $120 for the mandatory *four* tickets—no more, no less—as well as an $8 service charge. Very few fans could afford this outlay, and only about 10 percent of those who could would actually be selected to receive tickets; the rest would have to wait about four weeks for a refund.

Press criticism and public outrage were immediate, and when Michael received a letter from 11-year-old Ladonna Jones that criticized him for being "selfish," he decided enough was enough. At a July 5 press conference that was also attended by Marlon, Randy, and Tito on the day before the tour commenced, Michael announced that, instead of the mail-order ticketing system, fans would now be able to buy one or more tickets at the box office and that just under 2,000 tickets in each city would be provided free to underprivileged youths. What's more, he'd be donating his own tour earnings to charity. As a result, while Ladonna Jones received four complimentary tickets and was chauffeured to the show in a limousine, around $5 million was distributed among the T.J. Martell Foundation for Leukemia and Cancer Research, the United Negro College Fund, and the Ronald McDonald Camp for Good Times.

The unhappiness Michael (second from right) felt at being involved with the Victory tour was heightened by the controversy surrounding the sale of concert tickets.

November 30, 1984: Michael takes center stage at L.A.'s Dodger Stadium during the opening concert of the Victory tour's final leg.

"He dances with the breathtaking verve of his predecessor James Brown, the beguiling wispiness of Diana Ross, the ungainly pathos of Charlie Chaplin, the edgy joy of a man startled to be alive. The crowd gasps and screams, savoring not a fussy high-tech stage set but the grace and beauty of a brilliant entertainer."

—Music critic Jim Miller, Newsweek, July 7, 1984

"We Are the World"

In January 1985, immediately after the all-star Band Aid charity recording of "Do They Know It's Christmas?" had topped the UK singles chart for five weeks and raised millions of pounds for victims of the Ethiopian famine, actor/singer Harry Belafonte and fund-raiser Ken Kragen enlisted the help of Lionel Richie and Kenny Rogers to record an all-star American single benefiting Africa. When Richie contacted Michael Jackson, he said that he'd not only like to perform on the song but also help write it. The result was "We Are the World," which the pair completed at the Jackson family home on Hayvenhurst Avenue the night before its initial January 21 recording session at Kenny Rogers's Lion Share Recording Studio in Los Angeles. Coproduced by Quincy Jones and Michael Omartian and featuring Rogers, the cocomposers, and Stevie Wonder, this session was followed by an all-star get-together at Hollywood's A&M Recording Studios on January 28.

The finished record, credited to USA for Africa, was released on March 7 and became the fastest-selling pop single in American history, as well as the first to be certified multiplatinum en route to topping the Billboard Hot 100 and other charts around the world. The only track issued off the multistar *We Are the World* album, it scooped Grammy Awards for Record of the Year, Song of the Year, and Best Pop Performance by a Duo or Group with Vocal. As of 2009, "We Are the World" has sold more than 20 million units and raised over $63 million for humanitarian aid.

The fastest-selling American pop single in history, "We Are the World" earned four Grammy Awards at the ceremony held on February 25, 1986, including the one presented to Lionel Richie and MJ for Song of the Year.

USA for Africa

- Forty-four stars sang on "We Are the World," 21 of them performing solo vocals, while the rest were members of the chorus.
- The soloists included everyone from Tina Turner and Diana Ross to Bruce Springsteen and Bob Dylan.
- The chorus featured Band Aid organizer Bob Geldof, Smokey Robinson, and Bette Midler, as well as Jackson siblings Marlon, Randy, Tito, Jackie, and LaToya.
- Prince, having been invited to duet with MJ, was a no-show. Several reasons have been cited for this, including his wish to avoid working alongside other superstars and his annoyance at being called "a creep" by Geldof.

Although Michael was no longer around for the 2010 rerecording of "We Are the World," aiding victims of the Haiti earthquake, footage of him performing the song was included in the video.

clockwise from left Lionel Richie, Daryl Hall, Quincy Jones, Paul Simon, and Stevie Wonder during the "We Are the World" recording session on January 28, 1985.

"I did expect to see more ego. . . . You know, 'The Gloved One' meets 'The Boss' and things like that, but it's really not."

—*Paul Simon, Los Angeles Times, March 24, 1985*

Going for a Song:
The Beatles Catalog

In November 1981, showbiz impresario Sir Lew Grade informed Paul McCartney that he was thinking of selling ATV Music, which had acquired the Northern Songs publishing catalog of more than 250 John Lennon–Paul McCartney songs 12 years earlier. McCartney's offer of $20 million to purchase Northern Songs without the rest of ATV Music was rejected, and so in October 1984 he joined forces with Lennon's widow, Yoko Ono, to make a slightly higher offer for the entire company. McCartney just happened to tell Michael Jackson about this the following March, when Michael spent a weekend at McCartney's farm in the southern English county of Sussex. So, imagine McCartney's fury when, on August 10, 1985, it was announced that MJ had purchased ATV Music for $47.5 million, fending off strong bids by CBS, the Coca-Cola Corporation, EMI, and the Lawrence Welk Group.

While McCartney would subsequently insist he had no idea Michael had instructed his attorney John Branca to aggressively pursue ATV, the Jackson camp would claim that Branca had contacted McCartney's attorney and was informed that the Beatle wouldn't be bidding because the asking price was too high. Either way, a deal's a deal, and when, ten years later, Michael merged his ATV Music holdings with Sony Music Publishing, he received between

$90 and $110 million from Sony for a half stake in the ATV catalog that was by then estimated to be worth around $300 million. This figure would roughly double during the next decade, and by 2009 Michael would reportedly be earning about $75 million a year from the publishing partnership with Sony. All in all, MJ enjoyed quite a nice return on his original investment.

Although Paul McCartney appears shocked and Michael doesn't look too happy, MJ's reaction was likely quite the reverse when he learned his bid for The Beatles' song catalog had been successful.

Paul McCartney had greater music biz experience than Michael Jackson, but he was outmaneuvered by the younger man when it came to ownership of his own songs.

"We had a nice relationship, but Michael's the kind of guy who picks brains....I think it's slightly dodgy to do things like that—to be someone's friend and then to buy the rug they're standing on."

—Paul McCartney, Rolling Stone, *November/December 1987*

"It's just a great move, a corporate, entrepreneurial thing to do....It's about growth. Everything in life to me is about growth."

—Michael Jackson, after merging his ATV Music holdings with *Sony Music Publishing, USA Today, November 9, 1995*

Captain EO

Captain EO, under the leadership of Commander Bog and assisted by a motley crew of robots and aliens, navigates his spaceship toward a planet of dilapidated, twisted metal and steaming vents in order to deliver a gift to its Amazonian queen, the Supreme Leader.

Unfortunately, said leader isn't too friendly. So, after she sentences EO to 100 years of torture and demands that his crew be converted into trashcans, the good captain tries to conquer the queen and her Whip Warriors with music and dance. You can guess who wins this battle . . .

Executive produced by George Lucas; directed by Francis Ford Coppola; and starring MJ as EO, Anjelica Huston as the Supreme Leader, and Dick Shawn as

Commander Bog, this 17-minute 3-D space adventure cost a staggering $30 million to produce. The film opened on September 12, 1986, at Disney World's EPCOT Center as a "4-D" experience—the fourth "D" consisting of in-theater effects such as smoke and lasers. Featuring two of Michael's compositions, "We Are Here to Change the World" and "Another Part of Me," the movie was subsequently screened through the mid- to late 1990s at all of Disney's theme parks, where it has been revived since his death.

Although Michael didn't appear in many big-screen adventures, his performances always garnered plenty of attention, including his work in Captain EO *(opposite and right).*

"With acting, it's like becoming another person. I think that's neat, especially when you totally forget. If you totally forget, which I love to do, that's when it's magic. I love to create magic—to put something together that's so unusual, so unexpected that it blows people's heads off."

—*Michael Jackson*, Interview Magazine, *1982*

Michael, as Captain EO in the film of the same name, gets ready to deal with the Supreme Leader and her Whip Warriors.

Did You Know...?

- MJ's favorite Disneyland ride was "Pirates of the Caribbean."

- His drawing of Mickey Mouse was included in a 1991 book titled The Art of Mickey Mouse.

- On November 10, 1984, Michael received a star on Hollywood's Walk of Fame.

- During a visit to the Ivory Coast in 1992, he was crowned "King Sani" by a tribal chief and sat on a golden throne while presiding over ceremonial dances.

Included in The Art of Mickey Mouse, Michael's drawing of Disney's most famous creation was titled "Bad 1998." The sketch was his comic projection of how he would look as the "Bad" character in a few years' time.

HYPERBARIC CHAMBER

In September 1986, it was all over the news—the story that, in order to prolong his life, Michael Jackson was sleeping in a hyperbaric chamber. This casket-sized contraption, originally developed to treat scuba-diving disorders such as decompression sickness and gas embolism, encloses the patient in pure oxygen, which penetrates the body by way of higher-than-normal barometric pressure. While recuperating from the accident he'd suffered on the set of the Pepsi commercial, Michael had spotted one such machine at the Brotman Medical Center. Dr. Steven Hoefflin, a cosmetic surgeon at the center, told him of his theory that regularly sleeping in a hyperbaric chamber might increase a person's longevity. MJ immediately wanted to splash out $200,000 on one for himself. After a photo of MJ sleeping inside the chamber appeared on the front page of the *National Enquirer*, Frank DiLeo gave interviews to the press about how he and his "bizarre" client had been arguing about this "wacky" behavior.

Still, was it true? The giveaway was the photo, taken at Brotman in January 1984, which depicted Michael wearing street clothes without shoes instead of the requisite fire-retardant garments. However, in a *Boston Globe* interview in June 2009, author Stephen Davis said he saw the chamber at MJ's home when he was interviewing him for *Moon Walk*.

Regardless, this and other stunts—such as a subsequent report that MJ had offered the London Hospital Medical College a million dollars to purchase the bones of "Elephant Man" Joseph C. Merrick—would only backfire. Instead of making Michael appear a little more interesting, the rumors would cause him to forever be stuck with the tag of "Wacko Jacko" that was assigned to him by the British tabloid press.

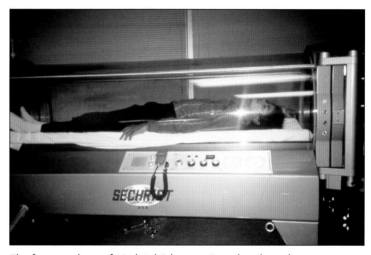

The famous photo of Michael "sleeping" inside a hyperbaric chamber was actually a publicity stunt, as indicated by MJ's lack of fire-retardant garments.

Bad

Michael Jackson, the biggest star of the 1980s, only released two studio albums during his halcyon decade. The first of these was *Thriller*—and, boy, was that a tough act to follow. Not that the other album, *Bad*, did too shabbily. Released on August 31, 1987, it sold eight million copies in the United States and more than 30 million worldwide and was the only album ever to spawn five Billboard Hot 100 chart toppers. Ten of the 11 tracks on *Bad* were actually issued as singles, the exception being "Just Good Friends" (featuring Stevie Wonder), which, along with "Man in the Mirror," was also one of only two songs on the album that Michael didn't compose. MJ coproduced his third and final collaboration with Quincy Jones, helping to give the record a harder edge than its predecessor in terms of rock and dance music, while still indulging his passions for mainstream pop and midtempo ballads. The result was generally favorable reviews, as well as Grammy Awards for Best Engineered Recording, Non-Classical, and Best Music Video-Short Form (for "Leave Me Alone").

Would you pick a fight with this guy? MJ's version of a street tough appeared on the cover of Bad.

"Michael Jackson: He's **Black.** He's *Bad.* Is This Guy Weird, or What?"

—People *headline, September 1987*

MJ's "bad boy" image onscreen and onstage was somewhat at odds with his proclamations of being "a lover not a fighter."

BY THE NUMBERS

The Music Videos
(1987–1989)

Year	Video	Director
1987	"Bad"	Martin Scorsese
	"The Way You Make Me Feel"	Joe Pytka
1988	"Man in the Mirror"	Donald Wilson
	"Dirty Diana"	Joe Pytka
	"Another Part of Me"	Patrick Kelly
	"Smooth Criminal"	Colin Chilvers
	"Speed Demon"	Colin Chilvers
	"Come Together"	Jerry Kramer & Colin Chilvers
	"Leave Me Alone"	Jim Blashfield & Paul Diener
1989	"Liberian Girl"	Jim Yukich

Big Bad Chart Toppers

- *"I Just Can't Stop Loving You,"* released July 20, 1987, was the first single from Bad as well as the first of five consecutive U.S. number ones. Initially intended to partner Michael with either Barbra Streisand or Whitney Houston, it ended up as a duet with singer-composer Siedah Garrett. Streisand thought her 16-year age difference with MJ wouldn't be appropriate, while Houston turned it down due to other commitments. Aretha Franklin and Abba's Agnetha Fältskog were also allegedly considered.

- The title track, originally conceived as a duet with Prince, debuted on September 7, 1987, and enhanced MJ's self-contrived badass image, as promoted in the accompanying Martin Scorsese–directed video.

- *"The Way You Make Me Feel"* came out on November 9, 1987, and hit the top spot on January 23 of the following year.

- *"Man in the Mirror"* was released on January 9, 1988, and featured backing vocals by Garrett, The Winans, and the gospel-laced Andraé Crouch Choir. Although written by Garrett and Glen Ballard, its

seemingly autobiographical lyrics have since made it one of Michael's theme songs.

■ The single "Dirty Diana," released April 18, 1988, was not, contrary to popular rumors, about either Diana Ross or Princess Diana but about the groupies that regularly hit on Michael and his brothers. Still, Princess Di did tell MJ that it was her favorite among his songs.

"Dirty Diana," "Man in the Mirror" (right), and "The Way You Make Me Feel" (above right) *were just three of the ten tracks off* Bad *to be issued as singles.*

The "Bad" Video

Bad was Michael Jackson's first album in five years, and there was almost as much hype preceding the world premiere of the title track's promo video as there once had been for *Gone with the Wind*. Or, at least, it seemed that way back in 1987. Directed by Martin Scorsese, choreographed by Jeffrey Daniel, and clearly influenced by the 1961 movie version of *West Side Story*, this 18-minute mini epic depicts a leather-clad punk named Daryl (MJ) reasserting himself among fellow gang members by leading them in an aggressive dance routine. One of the main participants is Mini Max, portrayed by a young Wesley Snipes, while the off-screen voice of Daryl's mother is provided by singer Roberta Flack. Filmed in both color and black-and-white, the music video was nominated for Best Choreography at the 1988 MTV Music Awards. "Bad" and MJ's other nominated video, "The Way You Make Me Feel," lost to "Pleasure Principle" by none other than Michael's kid sister, Janet.

MJ as a leather-clad punk showing some attitude in the "Bad" video directed by Martin Scorsese.

Smooth Moves

"Clean, neat, fast, with a sensuality that comes through," was how choreographer-director Bob Fosse described Michael Jackson's dancing talents in a March 19, 1984, article in *Time*, while Gene Kelly asserted, "He knows when to stop and then flash out like a bolt of lightning." Fred Astaire, to whom MJ dedicated his autobiography *Moon Walk*, went even further: "My Lord, he is a wonderful mover. He makes these moves up himself and is just wonderful to watch."

All his life, Michael learned from his dancing idols, borrowed some of their moves, and innovated his own, whether he was electrifying concert audiences or wowing viewers with music videos like "Smooth Criminal," the seventh single off the *Bad* album. In this short film, Michael, wearing a white suit and fedora, pays homage to Astaire in *The Band Wagon* while also executing his "anti-gravity lean." This was achieved by having shoes with ankle supports and cutouts in the heels that were temporarily attached to pegs rising from the stage at the appropriate moment. The effect was a seemingly impossible forward-sloping stance. The props were patented by MJ in October 1993.

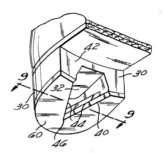

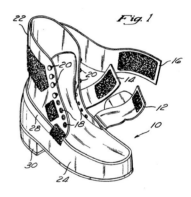

Fig. 1

While paying homage to Fred Astaire in his 1953 movie The Band Wagon *(above left), Michael used the "Smooth Criminal" video (left) to highlight his own innovative talents, executing the "anti-gravity lean" courtesy of the special shoes and stage props that he'd invented (above).*

Bad World Tour

- Michael's first world tour as a solo artist spanned the globe, with performances in Japan, Australia, the United States, Italy, Austria, the Netherlands, Sweden, Switzerland, Germany, France, England, Wales, Ireland, Spain, and Belgium between September 12, 1987, and January 27, 1989.

- Michael performed 123 shows in front of a record-breaking 4.4 million fans (The Rolling Stones' A Bigger Bang tour subsequently broke that record with 4.68 million tickets sold).

- Sponsored by Pepsi, the tour's total gross of $125 million was also a record at the time.

- While Michael donated some of his concert earnings to charitable causes, he also ensured that 400 tickets were provided to underprivileged children for each of his U.S. shows.

- Among the backup singers was a newcomer named Sheryl Crow, who would later have a successful career of her own, winning nine Grammy Awards as a solo artist. Crow performed the duet "I Just Can't Stop Loving You" with MJ during the concerts.

Before she became a star in her own right, singer-songwriter Sheryl Crow was a backing vocalist on the Bad world tour. In addition to dueting with MJ on "I Just Can't Stop Loving You," she was, according to tabloid newspaper the Globe, also carrying his baby...

Moon Walk

It was one thing to read the increasingly bizarre reports about Michael Jackson's behavior. However, when the pop phenom himself blew the lid off his private life—or, at least, certain aspects of it—in a supposed tell-all autobiography, it became an international best seller. His rise to fame, plastic surgery, female companions, and celebrity friends were all discussed in *Moon Walk*, published by Doubleday in February 1988 and edited by Jacqueline Kennedy Onassis, who also wrote the book's introduction. Still, by far the most explosive revelations were those of Michael being beaten by his father. He'd subsequently apologize to Joseph for this material, which, MJ assured him, had been written by somebody else. In truth, after manuscripts submitted by both music critic Robert Hilburn and rock author Stephen Davis hadn't met with the approval of either Michael or Doubleday, the pop star had authored the book himself, with help from editor Shaye Areheart. Topping the best-seller lists of the *New York Times, Los Angeles Times,* and the *Times* of London, *Moon Walk* quickly sold 450,000 copies worldwide.

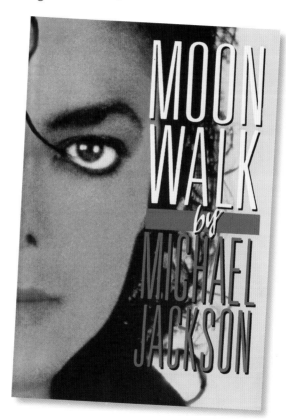

At a time when he could seemingly do no wrong, MJ even became a best-selling author.

Moonwalker

- Originally produced to coincide with the release of Bad, the movie Moonwalker was a collection of short stories about Michael Jackson, along with live performances and long-form music videos.

- Two "films within the film" were crafted around the songs "Speed Demon" and "Smooth Criminal," which features appearances by Sean Lennon and Joe Pesci as mobster Frankie LiDeo (a play on MJ's manager's name).

- Michael coproduced and codirected the movie, while also creating the storyline for "Smooth Criminal" and contributing much of the music alongside Bruce Broughton's score. The film also featured a performance by South African choral group Ladysmith Black Mambazo.

- Shot on a $60 million budget, Moonwalker was released in theaters in Europe and South America in October 1988 and then on home video in North America in January 1989.

- *Despite mixed reviews, the* Moonwalker *home video sold more than 800,000 copies in the United States within four months of its release.*
- *With Michael's help, Sega adapted* Moonwalker *into an arcade and home video game.*

A $60 million direct-to-video release, the movie Moonwalker nevertheless sold well and was adapted into a video game.

Neverland Valley Ranch

From 1988 until the end of his life, Michael's home in Santa Barbara County, California, was nearly as famous—and at the center of almost as many media reports—as the King of Pop himself. Originally called the Sycamore Valley Ranch, the 2,676-acre property was renamed Neverland by Michael in the spirit of the fictional world of Peter Pan, the boy who never grows up. He purchased the property from golf course developer William Bone for a reported $17 million—quite a bargain, in light of the $35 million asking price.

MJ had first fallen in love with the 13,000-square-foot house and surrounding land when it had been leased by Paul McCartney during the 1983 shoot of their "Say Say Say" music video. However, once he acquired it for himself, Michael turned it into not only his escape from the rest of the world but also his own private amusement park, featuring a clock made out of flowers, two railroads, a zoo, a Ferris wheel, a pirate ship, bumper cars, a carousel, a roller coaster, and assorted other rides. It was here that he welcomed groups of children, as well as their families; where his superstar friend Elizabeth Taylor married her eighth husband in October 1991; and where police raids investigating allegations of child sex abuse would prompt MJ to vacate the property in 2005, before financial pressures would force him to sell it three years later.

With its own private amusement park, the Neverland Ranch enabled Michael to live the kind of innocent, fun childhood that he had never experienced.

"I would like to see an international children's holiday to honor our children, because the family bond has been broken. . . . I hope that our next generation will get to see a peaceful world, not the way things are going now."

—Michael Jackson, Vibe, March 2002

Performing "Heal the World" with a South Korean children's choir during a visit to Seoul in October 1996, MJ communicated his hopes for a more peaceful world.

The Many Faces of Michael Jackson

In a widely seen February 1993 interview with Oprah Winfrey, Michael would assert that he'd only ever had two surgeries: rhinoplasty and a procedure to insert a cleft in his chin. However, the visual evidence suggested otherwise: His nose had been so emaciated by countless surgeries that it had collapsed, necessitating the insertion of new cartilage into the tip. Then, when this wasn't successful, he'd taken to allegedly wearing a prosthetic nose-tip that he camouflaged with makeup. What's more, he had thinner, tattooed lips; higher cheekbones; and increasingly paler skin. Diagnosed during the 1980s with the skin-lightening disease vitiligo (which may well have been caused by his use of facial bleaching chemicals) and discoid lupus on his scalp, Michael used skin-lightening creams as part-treatment, part-makeup and also resorted to hats and umbrellas outside to protect himself from sunlight.

The nose and lips get thinner, the cheekbones get higher, the skin gets lighter, the eyebrows get more arched, and the chin acquires a dimple—it is anyone's guess as to how much cosmetic surgery Michael truly underwent.

DIANA'S LOOK

Okay, so Michael admired and adored Diana Ross, and facial surgeries through the mid-1980s that left him with arched eyebrows, higher cheekbones, and a slimmer nose did create a noticeable resemblance to the former Supreme. But despite all of the press assertions and public speculation, did he *really* want to look like her? The answer, apparently, was no, as evidenced by Michael's cleft chin and subsequent cosmetic adjustments. Still, *you* decide . . .

Separated at birth? Not quite, but after all of his facial changes Michael did share some striking similarities with Diana Ross.

A Renewed Contract

By 1990 Michael's contract with CBS Records had expired, yet he still owed the label four more albums. This meant that, if he signed with another company, CBS could sue him for the estimated loss of profits. Still, David Geffen, who owned his own record label, tried to persuade MJ to jump ship and not worry

Although he convinced Michael (pictured here between Liza Minnelli and Quincy Jones) *that he needed to secure a better record deal, David Geffen* (left) *didn't persuade MJ to sign with Geffen's label.*

about the consequences; Michael's lawyer, John Branca, strongly disagreed. Geffen's opinion ultimately convinced MJ that he deserved a better record deal, despite the fact that he already had one of the best deals in the industry—one that had been negotiated for him by Branca and had made Michael extremely wealthy. The result was the temporary end of the Jackson/Branca relationship and a renegotiated 15-year, six-album contract with Sony (formerly CBS) that provided Michael with a nonrefundable $3 million signing bonus and an unprecedented 25 percent royalty on album sales. This would eventually earn him an estimated $175 million.

Hobbies and Interests

Reading

Collecting artwork

Shopping

Drawing

Painting

Video games

Collecting movie memorabilia and old costumes

Amusement park rides

Martial arts

Philanthropic/humanitarian causes

above left **A young MJ displaying some of his artwork.** *above right* **Many organizations benefited from Michael's generosity, including the United Negro College Fund.**

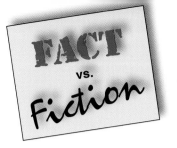

MJ'S APPEARANCE ON *THE SIMPSONS*

When "Stark Raving Dad," the premier episode of the third season of *The Simpsons* aired on the Fox network on September 19, 1991, viewers may have recognized the voice of the man with whom Homer shares a room when he's sent to a mental institution. While Homer is there after being mistaken for a "free-thinking anarchist" because he's

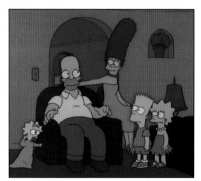

MJ joined the famous cartoon family for an episode as a bald, overweight Leon Kompowsky.

wearing a pink shirt, his roommate Leon Kompowsky, despite being white, bald, and overweight, behaves like he's Michael Jackson. MJ, a huge fan of the show, offered to make a guest appearance in addition to contributing script ideas, speaking Leon's lines, and even writing the song "Happy Birthday Lisa" (which was performed by MJ soundalike Kipp Lennon). However, for contractual reasons Michael's name couldn't be used, so Leon's voice was credited to "John Jay Smith." Only later was it confirmed that MJ had indeed voiced the role.

Dangerous

- Recorded in Los Angeles between June 1990 and October 1991, Dangerous *was by far the lengthiest album project that Michael had been involved with up until that time.*

- *Michael shared production credits with "King of New Jack Swing" Teddy Riley and critically acclaimed songwriter-producer Bill Bottrell on the tracks he cowrote with them.*

- *Released on November 26, 1991, with a 77-minute running time that could be accommodated by the industry's new CD format,* Dangerous *was also issued as a double LP on vinyl.*

- *A chart topper on both sides of the Atlantic,* Dangerous *was MJ's fastest-selling album in the United States and the first to spawn seven Top Ten singles in the UK.*

- *Michael's second album to debut atop the Billboard 200,* Dangerous *has, to date, sold more than 32 million copies worldwide, making it his second-best-selling record behind* Thriller.

Designed by surrealist pop artist Mark Ryden, the mysterious cover for Dangerous contained various Masonic occult symbols and is a topic of debate to this day.

"Black or White"

Among the main themes running through Michael Jackson's solo career, his message of racial harmony was the most prominent. So, it was fitting that the lead single off the *Dangerous* album—and his first of the 1990s—was "Black or White," an infectious "rock 'n' roll dance song" (as described by Epic's publicity material) that he co-wrote with Bill Bottrell. Bottrell also engineered the track and contributed its rap lyrics, percussion, and guitar solo; Guns N' Roses guitarist Slash played the solo. An international chart topper, it spent seven weeks at No. 1 in the United States and became the first American single to enter the UK chart in that position since Elvis Presley's "It's Now or Never" in 1960. Then again, "Black or White" was also greatly assisted by the simultaneous TV premiere of its groundbreaking video on November 14, 1991. Directed by Jon Landis (the man who had helmed the "Thriller" video), it featured everyone from child actor Macaulay Culkin to supermodel Tyra Banks and ended with a then-stunning segment in which people of different races and genders morphed into one another. An estimated 500 million viewers in 27 countries tuned in to the premiere.

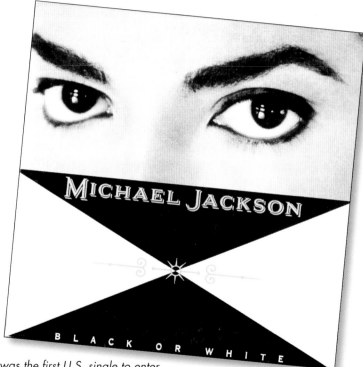

"Black or White" was the first U.S. single to enter the British chart at No. 1 in more than 30 years, and its groundbreaking video attracted a massive worldwide audience.

Dangerous World Tour

It was at the start of the third phase of the Dangerous tour that Michael's world began to be ripped apart by scandal. Here, he's seen performing at London's Wembley Stadium on July 30, 1992, during the tour's initial leg.

- *Again sponsored by Pepsi and running from June 27, 1992, to November 11, 1993, Michael's second solo world tour comprised 69 concerts in front of 3.9 million fans in 26 countries.*

- *The tour grossed about $125 million, and Michael donated all profits to various charities, including his new Heal the World Foundation.*

- *In the middle of the third leg, which commenced August 24, 1993, Michael ended the tour without having performed in the United States or Canada.*

- *Michael's reasons included his suffering from dehydration, migraines, and back aches, as well as a dependence on painkillers and stress due to the concurrent accusation of child molestation.*

Heal the World Foundation

Founded in 1992, Michael's Heal the World Foundation took its name from the song of hope that was issued as a single off of the *Dangerous* album. The charity's mission was to provide underprivileged children with food and medicine while helping them fight homelessness, exploitation, and abuse. Thanks to all of the money raised by the *Dangerous* world tour, the Heal the World Foundation was able to airlift 46 tons of supplies to war-torn Sarajevo as well as pay for a Hungarian child's liver transplant. Education about drug and alcohol abuse was also part of the organization's agenda, as were visits for underprivileged children to the theme park on Michael's Neverland Ranch.

Michael was never happier than when in the company of children, but this also gave rise to rumors and accusations.

A Family of Friends

- *Child actors Emmanuel Lewis and Macaulay Culkin*
- *Actors Tatum O'Neal, Brooke Shields, Jane Fonda, and Elizabeth Taylor*

Whether spending time with Elizabeth Taylor and Macaulay Culkin (top right) in 2001, Tatum O'Neal (bottom left) in 1979, or Jane Fonda (bottom right) in 1983, Michael enjoyed the company of a select circle of celebrity friends.

"We had a bond, and maybe it was because we both understood what it was like to be in the spotlight at a very young age."

—Brooke Shields, at MJ's memorial service, July 7, 2009

February 28, 1984: Following the 26th annual Grammy Awards show, MJ attended a party at Jimmy's restaurant in Beverly Hills with Brooke Shields and Emmanuel Lewis.

MJ and Liz

Their friendship began in an unconventional way. But then, they were unconventional people. Michael Jackson had admired screen goddess Elizabeth Taylor since he was a child. So, when he learned that Liz had walked out on one of his shows, he phoned her in tears to ask why. She informed him that her departure had been due to poor visibility, not his performance. That short call turned into a three-hour conversation, and so began a close relationship that was founded on the things the pair had in common. Both former juvenile stars felt like they had been deprived of their childhoods, and they knew the privileges and pitfalls of being a celebrity. Out of their shared feelings and common experiences, they formed a lasting bond of trust and companionship while doing their best to support charitable causes.

On February 16, 1997, Michael attended Liz Taylor's 65th birthday party, which was an AIDS benefit staged inside L.A.'s Pantages Theater.

"I don't think anyone knew how much we loved each other.
The purest, most giving love I've ever known."

—*Elizabeth Taylor on Michael Jackson, People, June 26, 2009*

Super Bowl XXVII

- *Super Bowl XXVII saw the Dallas Cowboys defeat the Buffalo Bills at the Rose Bowl in Pasadena, California, on January 31, 1993.*

- *Michael performed the entire halftime show, and it was one of the few times people tuned in at halftime to see a single entertainer.*

- *Following declining viewer numbers in recent years, the 1993 game was the first Super Bowl in which TV viewership actually increased during the halftime show.*

- *MJ made his grand entrance by being catapulted onto the stage before launching into a set that included "Jam," "Billie Jean," and "Black or White."*

- *Following a video montage depicting Michael's involvement with various humanitarian causes, the finale featured a group of 3,500 L.A. children singing "We Are the World" and backing Michael on "Heal the World."*

After being catapulted onto the stage and striking one of his trademark poses (above), MJ sang several of his hits and performed with L.A. children (left) during the Super Bowl XXVII halftime show.

Jordan Chandler Scandal

Michael first befriended Jordan Chandler in 1984, when he called the four-year-old to thank him for a get-well note Jordie had sent MJ while he was recuperating in the hospital after the Pepsi commercial debacle. Michael and Jordie then reconnected in 1992 when MJ visited the rental car facility of Jordie's step-father, met the 12-year-old, and took his phone number. Their close friendship soon became public knowledge, courtesy of tabloids reporting on how MJ and Jordie went everywhere together and how Michael had become like a member of the Chandler family.

In August 1993, after Jordie's father, Evan, instigated criminal proceedings against Michael for allegedly molesting his child, the police attained a warrant to search the Neverland Ranch and interviewed many other children who had stayed there. That December, MJ was strip-searched by police, and on the 22nd he responded with a TV statement broadcast live from Neverland in which he denied all charges. At a time when the scandal sent Michael's popularity into sharp decline, a poll conducted by TV show *A Current Affair* found that 75 percent of the people who saw his statement believed his denials. Still, in the face of incessantly negative media coverage and people selling damning stories about Michael to the tabloids, his insurance company agreed to an out-of-court settlement in the civil case filed by the Chandlers to the tune of $22 million. Jordie then refused to testify at the criminal trial, and those charges were dropped.

A frame grab from a video shows Michael with Jordan Chandler at a Las Vegas hotel in early 1993.

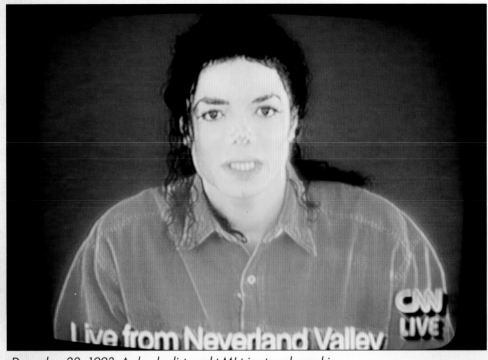

December 22, 1993: A clearly distraught MJ tries to salvage his reputation with a statement broadcast live from Neverland Ranch.

"I ask all of you to wait and hear the truth before you condemn me. Don't treat me like a criminal, because I am innocent."

—Michael Jackson, December 22, 1993

BY THE NUMBERS

The Music Videos
(1991–1993)

Year	Video	Director
1991	"Black or White"	John Landis
1992	"Remember the Time"	John Singleton
	"In the Closet"	Herb Ritts
	"Jam"	Michael Jackson & David Kellogg
	"Heal the World"	Joe Pytka
1993	"Give In to Me"	Andy Moharan
	"Who Is It"	David Fincher
	"Will You Be There"	Vincent Paterson
	"Gone Too Soon"	Bill DiCicco

Chapter 5

"Gone Too Soon"—
Broken Image, Tragic End

"I'm a strong person, I'm a warrior, and I know what's inside of me. I'm a fighter, but it's very painful. At the end of the day...
I'm still a human being."

—Michael Jackson, 2005, on Jesse Jackson's Keep Hope Alive radio show

Michael performs "Billie Jean" during the
12th annual MTV Video Music Awards show at
New York's Radio City Music Hall, September 7, 1995.

A Royal Couple

In February 1968, just as nine-year-old Michael Jackson, the future King of Pop, stood on the cusp of worldwide fame, another member of rock royalty was born in Memphis, Tennessee: Lisa Marie Presley, the only child of the King of Rock 'n' Roll, Elvis Presley, and his wife, Priscilla. Just over a quarter century later, Lisa Marie and MJ united for a marriage that shocked the world. The so-called Princess of Pop divorced her first husband, musician Danny Keough, just 20 days before she and Michael wed on May 26, 1994. In

light of the child molestation scandal then surrounding MJ, as well as the ongoing debate about his sexuality, many people wondered what Lisa Marie could possibly be thinking. To them, the marriage was Michael's transparent attempt to repair his image. Yet, according to Lisa Marie, the Jackson-Presley relationship was far from a sham.

After their first date at a mutual friend's dinner party, the couple realized they had much in common, not the least their unconventional childhoods and disconnection from the real world. Lisa Marie was attracted to offbeat guys, and few were as offbeat as Michael. MJ, meanwhile, was physically attracted to Elvis's daughter and found a sympathetic ear during the aforementioned child abuse scandal. Following a whirlwind romance, they wed at a secret ceremony in the Dominican Republic, and thereafter Lisa Marie helped persuade Michael to avoid further heartache by settling the case with Jordan Chandler. Still, she couldn't dissuade him from taking drugs to alleviate his physical and emotional pain, indulging in wild mood swings, or continuing to hang out with young boys. So, when Lisa Marie balked at the idea of starting a family with Michael, despite his burning desire to become a father, their relationship quickly unraveled.

From opening the 1994 MTV Video Music Awards show by planting a kiss on Lisa Marie's lips (opposite) to strolling hand-in-hand with her in front of press photographers at the Neverland Ranch seven months later (right), MJ made it clear there was passion aplenty in their relationship.

HIStory—Past, Present and Future, Book 1

■ Released on June 16, 1995, the HIStory double album combined 15 of Michael's greatest solo hits with 15 new tracks.

■ The album produced five singles: "Scream," which Michael performed with his sister Janet, was his response to being misrepresented by the tabloid press; "You Are Not Alone," which was written by R&B star R. Kelly; "Earth Song," which topped the UK chart and became his best-selling release there; "They Don't Care About Us," which went Top Ten in 14 countries; and "Stranger in Moscow," which, like "Earth Song" and "They Don't Care About Us," was far more successful overseas than in the United States.

■ The futuristic "Scream" video, featuring Michael and Janet, was shot on a $7 million budget that still distinguishes it as the most expensive music video ever made.

■ As of 2010, HIStory has sold more than 20 million copies worldwide and is the best-selling multiple-disc album of all time by a solo artist.

■ Blood on the Dance Floor: HIStory in the Mix, *released in 1997, contains remixes of the hit singles as well as five new songs. Worldwide sales of six million copies make it the most successful remix album ever released.*

In June 1995, as part of a $30 million publicity campaign for the HIStory album, Sony built nine 32-foot-tall steel-and-fiberglass statues like the one on the album cover and placed them strategically in cities around Europe. The statue in London was floated on a barge down the River Thames.

HIStory World Tour

- Running from September 7, 1996, to October 15, 1997, this was the third and—as it would turn out—final concert tour completed by Michael Jackson.

- Michael performed in more than 20 countries around the world, including the Czech Republic, Russia, Poland, Spain, the Netherlands, Tunisia, South Korea, Malaysia, India, Thailand, New Zealand, Australia, the Philippines, Japan, Germany, Italy, Switzerland, France, Austria, the United Kingdom, Ireland, Denmark, Sweden, Norway, Finland, Belgium, and South Africa.

The first leg of MJ's final concert tour included shows in Singapore (above) and Taiwan (opposite). His costume was designed by Gianni Versace.

- MJ's only U.S. shows on this tour were in Hawaii. He didn't perform on the American mainland.

- A then-record-breaking 4.5 million fans paid a total of $165 million to see the 82 shows.

"You Are Not Alone"

Written and coproduced by R&B artist R. Kelly, who incidentally would soon be involved in his own child sex scandals, "You Are Not Alone" was the first song ever to enter the Billboard Hot 100 at No. 1. This ballad about love and separation would also be Michael's last U.S. chart-topper during his lifetime. The promotional video, which featured a shorthaired MJ performing the song in an empty concert venue and other isolated settings, also depicted him and Lisa Marie canoodling seminude in a heavenly temple. The celestial theme was then underscored by Michael's appearance as a feathery-winged angel in the extended version of the film that was included on the 1997 video compilation *HIStory on Film, Volume II*. Following the couple's January 18, 1996, divorce, Lisa Marie said in *Michael Jackson: The Magic, The Madness, The Whole Story* that she only participated because she was "sucked up in the moment. It was kind of cool being in a Michael Jackson video."

The "You Are Not Alone" video featured a shorthaired MJ cavorting seminude with his famous wife. However, just before it first aired on TV, computer effects were used to conceal the fact that, in one scene, Michael was completely naked.

BY THE NUMBERS

The Music Videos
(1995–2009)

Year	Video	Director
1995	"HIStory Teaser"	Rupert Wainwright
	"Scream"	Mark Romanek
	"Childhood"	Nicholas Brandt
	"You Are Not Alone"	Wayne Isham
	"Earth Song"	Nicholas Brandt
1996	"They Don't Care About Us"	Spike Lee
	"Stranger in Moscow"	Nicholas Brandt
1997	"Blood on the Dance Floor"	Michael Jackson & Vincent Paterson
	"Ghosts"	Stan Winston
2001	"You Rock My World"	Paul Hunter
	"Cry"	Nicholas Brandt
2009	"This Is It"	Spike Lee

King of Bling

From gold braid and sequins to red leather and multicolored spangles, the King of Pop was also the King of Bling.

"[Michael Jackson] was 'the King of Bling' before the term 'bling' even existed."

—*Celebrity stylist Phillip Bloch, StyleList, June 26, 2009*

"Scream"

Fed up with the bashing that Michael had been receiving from the media, he and his sister Janet get away from Earth aboard a vast, futuristic, sparsely furnished spacecraft. That was the basic premise created by director Mark Romanek for the "Scream" video, which, as designed by Tom Foden and choreographed by Travis Payne, LaVelle Smith Jr., Sean Cheesman, and Tina Landon, featured the siblings venting their anger, playing video games, and dancing all over the 13-piece set that had been dreamed up by art directors Richard Berg, Jeff Hall, and Martin Mervel. Executing his trademark spins while also robot dancing and moonwalking, Michael hadn't, for once, been involved in the video's conception, yet it won 3 of the 11 MTV Video Music Awards for which it was nominated, as well as the Grammy for Best Short-Form Music Video. Premiering in the summer of 1995 on MTV and BET, it was also seen by an estimated

64 million viewers when aired alongside Diane Sawyer's interview with MJ and Lisa Marie Presley on ABC-TV's *Primetime Live.*

"It was great, because we love to dance, and to get in a room and dance with my sister reminds me of old times. . . . It allowed us to play and goof off and throw stuff. It was fun."

—*Michael Jackson on MTV, 1995*

The "Scream" video had MJ and Janet in spacesuit-type outfits and featured a variety of pop culture references.

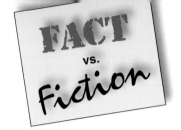

MASKED MAN

As the 1990s commenced, Michael began making public appearances wearing a surgical mask that covered his nose and mouth. The mask, of course, only served to fuel the flames of conjecture about his increasingly bizarre behavior, tying in perfectly with press speculation that he was turning into the "Howard Hughes of Pop"—an immensely wealthy yet reclusive hypochondriac. As it happens, although Michael was mega rich, he was anything but reclusive, entertaining numerous visitors at his Neverland Ranch while frequently venturing out in public—which is why the paparazzi were so often able to snap photos of him in his masks. Still, the debate continues as to whether the masks' purpose was to conceal the scars of his latest cosmetic surgery, protect him from airborne germs, guard against respiratory problems caused by a rare lung disease, or simply attract attention by looking plain weird.

The surgical masks that Michael wore to cover his nose and mouth were often designer masks, many of them created by his longtime costume designers Michael Bush and Dennis Tompkins.

Ghosts

Starring Michael Jackson, who also coproduced the movie, wrote the music, and conceived the story with Stephen King, *Ghosts* was a 39-minute film about a freaky-looking Maestro (MJ) with supernatural powers who is branded a "weirdo" by the inhabitants of Normal Valley. This is after they learn he's been scaring their kids with his offbeat magical tricks.

Led by the Mayor (also played by Michael) and armed with flaming torches in true horror film fashion, the Normal Valley horde visits the Maestro's creepy mansion and tell him to leave town. The Maestro's response is to pull some shocking magic stunts, such as stretching his own face and pulling it off to reveal his skull, before dancing with his "family" of ghouls and forcing the Mayor to join in.

Ultimately, it is the terrified Mayor who flees town, having been transformed into a grotesque-looking demon while being asked, "Who's the freak now?"

Directed by Academy Award–winning special effects whiz Stan Winston—acclaimed for his work on the *Terminator* and *Jurassic Park* films—*Ghosts* featured the songs "2 Bad," "Ghosts," and "Is It Scary" from Michael's *HIStory* and *Blood on the Dance Floor: HIStory in the Mix* albums. First screened in 1996 and released on video a year later, it set a Guinness World Record in 2002 as the Longest Music Video ever made. Viewers get to see MJ performing as several of the dancing ghouls, as well as an early film appearance by rapper Mos Def.

right **MJ arrives at Cannes' Festival Palace for a screening of** Ghosts **on May 9, 1997.**
opposite **The longest music video ever made,** Ghosts **was presented at the 50th Cannes Film Festival but was not one of the 20 movies selected to compete for the event's grand prize.**

Debbie Rowe

One of the final nails in the coffin of Michael's marriage to Lisa Marie Presley was his assertion that, if she didn't want to have children with him, he knew someone who did. That person was Debbie Rowe, a nurse in the office of dermatologist Dr. Arnold Klein, who had been treating Michael for his vitiligo skin disorder. A longtime MJ fan, Rowe was happy to accommodate his parental need. So, on November 14, 1996, they married in Sydney, Australia, 11 months after Michael's divorce

Debbie Rowe was completely different in terms of looks and personality than the first Mrs. Michael Jackson.

from Lisa Marie and ten days after his announcement that Rowe was carrying his child. You can imagine how the press and public doubted *that* claim. Yet, on February 13, 1997, Rowe gave birth to Michael Joseph Jackson Jr. and provided him with a sister, Paris-Michael Katherine Jackson, the following year. Since Michael chose to raise the children alone, they initially didn't even know Rowe was their mother. She granted MJ full custody after their October 1999 divorce.

"Debbie and I love each other for all the things you'll never see on stage or in pictures. I fell for the beautiful, unpretentious, giving person that she is, and she fell for me just being me."

—Michael Jackson,
OK! magazine, March 1997

From the very start, the Jackson-Rowe relationship was a little strange, and the ramifications of their unusual arrangement would continue after Michael's death, including disputes over her custody and visitation rights.

Prince, Paris & Blanket

- *Michael Joseph Jackson Jr., born February 13, 1997, was called Prince by Michael, who told OK! magazine, "My grandfather and great-grandfather were both named Prince, so we have carried on the tradition."*

- *Paris-Michael Katherine Jackson was born April 3, 1998.*

- *Prince Michael Jackson II was born February 21, 2002. Nicknamed "Blanket," he was, according to MJ, the result of the artificial insemination of an unidentified surrogate mother.*

- *In his UK television interview with Martin Bashir, Michael explained that "blanket" was his expression for a blessing.*

Michael didn't mind making public appearances with his kids... so long as their faces were covered.

SPOTLIGHT ON

Invincible

Michael started recording his tenth and final studio album in October 1997 and didn't complete the track "You Are My Life" until just eight weeks before *Invincible* was released in October 2001. Rodney Jerkins, Teddy Riley, Kenneth "Babyface" Edmonds, and R. Kelly were among the songwriters

Since Michael's final album took nearly four years to record and cost about $30 million to produce, worldwide sales figures of 10 million copies were actually a little disappointing.

who also shared production credits with MJ. The result was an album that topped the charts in 13 countries, including the United States, France, and Australia, en route to selling an estimated 10 million copies worldwide. Because the album cost a reported $30 million to produce, its sales figures were actually disappointing compared to those of Michael's previous albums. Furthermore, while the critics' reviews were generally favorable, there was a consensus that, with a playing time in excess of 77 minutes, the record was just too long.

"The record companies really, really do **conspire** against the artists. They **steal**, they **cheat**, they do whatever they can."

—Michael Jackson, June 2002,
after a dispute with Sony
had led to him quitting the label

MJ expresses his feelings about Sony Records chairman Tommy Mottola during a demonstration outside the company's headquarters in New York City in 2002.

Invincible Singles

- Only three tracks from Invincible were issued as singles: "You Rock My World"; "Butterflies"; and "Cry," which was never released in the United States.

- Debuting in August 2001, "You Rock My World" peaked at No. 10 on the Billboard Hot 100, making it Michael's first Top Ten single in America in more than six years, as well as the last during his lifetime.

- Due to Sony's subsequent boycotting of the album, "You Rock My World" was the only single to have a promo video featuring Michael. It was the last one in which he would appear.

top "You Rock My World" was Michael's final Top Ten U.S. single during his lifetime. *bottom* The single "Butterflies" didn't do so bad itself, reaching No. 14 on the charts.

- *Released in December 2001, "Butterflies" peaked at No. 14 on the Billboard Hot 100.*
- *Released outside the United States in November 2001, "Cry" peaked at No. 25 in the UK. Its highest chart position was No. 16 in the Netherlands.*

Costarring Marlon Brando, Chris Tucker, and Michael Madsen, the storyline of the "You Rock My World" video was somewhat related to "Smooth Criminal." The video was the last to feature MJ's active participation.

30th Anniversary Celebration

In September 2001, two concerts were staged at New York's Madison Square Garden to honor Michael's 30th anniversary as a solo artist.

The shows featured contributions by performers such as Whitney Houston, Liza Minnelli, James Ingram, Gloria Estefan, and Marc Anthony, as well as Michael's first onstage appearance with The Jacksons since 1984.

Ticket prices were the most expensive ever for a pop concert, topping out at $5,000 for a seat, dinner with MJ, and a signed poster. Michael himself earned $15 million for the two shows.

The shows were edited into a two-hour TV special titled *Michael Jackson: 30th Anniversary Celebration—The Solo Years,* which aired that November.

The second show took place the night before the 9/11 terrorist attacks, after which Michael helped organize the *United We Stand: What More Can I Give* all-star benefit concert at RFK Stadium in Washington, D.C.

While Michael performed with N'Sync (left) during his "30th Anniversary Celebration," the collaborative highlight was his first onstage performance with Jermaine and the other members of The Jacksons since 1984 (right).

Bubbles the Chimp

He slept in a crib in Michael's bedroom, used the pop star's private toilet, accompanied him on tour, had his own agent, took instructions on how to moonwalk, and was even rumored to be the potential ring bearer for Liz Taylor's eighth wedding at the Neverland Ranch. His name was Bubbles, and if the tabloids ever needed material to forge and embellish the image of "Wacko Jacko," they found it in the chimp Michael rescued from a Texas research facility in mid-1985. The two of them even wore matching outfits! Bubbles resided at the Jackson family home in Encino before moving to Neverland in 1988. Shortly after, he was one of many celebrities to appear in the music video for "Liberian Girl," a single off Michael's *Bad* album. However, the relationship turned sour when Bubbles became overly aggressive. Shipped off to the Sylmar, California, ranch of animal trainer Bob Dunne, Bubbles reportedly attempted suicide there in late 2003 and has resided at the Center for Great Apes in Wauchula, Florida, since 2004. He didn't attend Michael's memorial service, but LaToya reconnected with the chimp in 2010 for the Animal Planet documentary *Michael Jackson and Bubbles: The Untold Story.*

Bubbles displaying a sharp sense of fashion and impeccable table manners in front of the press.

Blanket and the Balcony

On November 19, 2002, Michael was in Germany to accept a Bambi Lifetime Achievement Award for his philanthropic work on behalf of children. This was perceived as somewhat misguided in light of how he handled one of his own kids—quite literally—while staying at Berlin's Hotel Adlon. In an apparent gesture of goodwill toward his fans and the news cameras gathered in the street below, Michael dangled nine-month-old Blanket over the fourth-floor balcony of his room, gripping the baby—whose face was concealed by a towel over his head—with just one arm around the waist. While some fans cheered, others screamed, and the next day the incident made newspaper headlines around the world. "You Lunatic!" screamed UK tabloid *The Sun,* while Britain's *Daily Mirror* accused MJ of being a "Mad Bad Dad." Michael quickly issued a statement admitting he had made a "terrible mistake."

Don't try this at home: MJ may have kept a tight grip on Blanket while dangling the baby over his hotel balcony, but even photos of the incident made some people break into a sweat.

Living with Michael Jackson

By 2003, Michael was no stranger to bad press, what with the lingering child molestation rumors; his dangling of Blanket over that Berlin hotel balcony; and his constantly evolving, cosmetically altered features. Yet he suffered possibly his greatest public relations disaster at the hands of British journalist Martin Bashir in February of that year. Over the course of eight months, Bashir interviewed MJ at Neverland, as well as in Las Vegas, Berlin, and Miami, for a documentary titled *Living with Michael Jackson* that provided TV viewers with unprecedented insight into its subject's private world. However, after the show aired on Britain's ITV network on February 3 and on ABC in the United States just three days later, all hell broke loose over what many perceived to be Michael's disturbing fathering of his kids, including bottle-feeding a masked Blanket on his juddering knee and making incendiary statements about how he still allowed children to sleep in his bed while he slept on the floor.

Bashir's voice-over narrative was often critical of Michael, as were many of the two-hour documentary's 38 million American and 15 million British viewers. Michael's response was to issue *Take Two: The Footage You Were Never Meant to See* a few weeks later for broadcast on the Fox network. Presented by talk show host Maury Povich, this rebuttal video featured outtake footage from the Bashir documentary, including interview material in which the journalist actually praised MJ for his parenting skills and for inviting children to Neverland. (In the documentary, Bashir had described Michael's home as a "dangerous place" for kids.) Further damage control was attempted via new interviews with Jackson intimates such as Debbie Rowe, who defended his actions. The fallout continued, however, when one of the children in the documentary, 13-year-old Gavin Arvizo—who was seen holding Michael's hand and resting his head on his shoulder—accused Michael of sexual abuse soon after the piece aired. Although Michael would be acquitted of all charges two years later in a highly publicized court case, strong doubts would remain.

left An artist's rendition of outtake footage from Martin Bashir's TV documentary being viewed as evidence during Michael's child molestation trial in May 2005. The documentary itself had already been issued on DVD. *right* Gavin Arvizo, pictured here with MJ in Living with Michael Jackson, would later accuse the pop star of sexual abuse.

Cameo Appearances

- *Michael Jackson made cameo appearances in two feature films at the start of the 21st century: Men in Black II (2002), starring Will Smith and Tommy Lee Jones, and Miss Cast Away & the Island Girls (2004), starring Eric Roberts and Charlie Schlatter.*

- *In the sci-fi action comedy Men in Black II, MJ plays himself, trying to persuade Chief Zed (Rip Torn) to make him Agent M.*

- *In the B-movie spoof Miss Cast Away & the Island Girls, a plane carrying beauty contestants crash-lands on a desert island, leaving the pilots to protect them from alien apes and a gigantic prehistoric pig named Jurassic Pork. Michael plays Agent MJ, a representative of the Vatican. (Don't ask why... it was that kind of a movie.)*

- *Michael's Miss Cast Away scenes were shot at Neverland, where the tooting horn of the theme park train interrupted filming.*

- *The bad publicity emanating from Michael's legal problems caused the postponement of the scheduled summer release of Miss Cast Away to movie theaters. In the end, the film went straight to DVD in July 2005.*

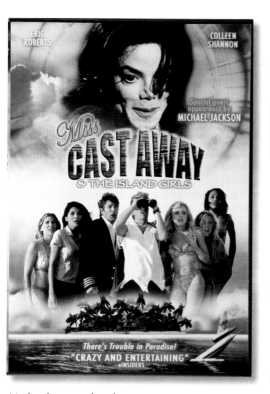

Michael enjoyed making movie appearances, but his project choices were sometimes questionable. "Tropical-island trash" is how a critic for the *Washington Post* described *Miss Cast Away & the Island Girls* while noting that MJ "does the most convincing acting job of the entire cast, which, of course, isn't saying much."

Sheikh Abdulla Bin Hamad Bin Isa Al-Khalifa

When his world was falling apart amid renewed charges of child molestation, the King of Pop turned to a Bahraini prince for some much needed help. The second son of the King of Bahrain, as well as a music aficionado and a friend of Michael and Jermaine since 2004, Sheikh Abdulla Bin Hamad Bin Isa Al-Khalifa loaned MJ approximately $3.3 million to help pay his legal fees. Then, on June 30 of that year, after the charges against him had been dropped, Michael accepted

Sheikh Abdulla's offer for him, his children, and his personal staff to be the prince's guests in Bahrain. In return, Michael agreed to record a song, "I Have This Dream," which Sheikh Abdulla had written as a charity single for Hurricane Katrina victims.

In November 2008, the sheikh sued Michael for $7 million, claiming that the single had never been released because Michael had failed to attend the final session. He also charged that MJ had reneged on a contract for a new album, an autobiography, and a stage play. According to Sheikh Abdulla, he had covered MJ's living and travel expenses, built him a studio in one of his palaces, spent more than $300,000 for him to consult a "motivational guru," and provided him with a $250,000 cash loan to "entertain his friends at Christmas." Michael claimed these were gifts, though he eventually settled out of court.

Aside from hobnobbing with the king of Bahrain while living as the house guest of the royal ruler's second-eldest son (opposite), *the King of Pop took advantage of the opportunity to hide behind some traditional clothing by wearing an* abaya, *which is a woman's veil and gown* (above).

Financial Woes

- In March 2006, the main house at Neverland was closed to cut costs.

- Michael had been delinquent on his repayment of a $270 million loan that had been secured against his music publishing interests, even though those interests were reportedly earning him up to $75 million a year.

The train station at Neverland Ranch, shown here in 2003, was eventually closed down along with the rest of the property when Michael found himself in a financial hole. He sold the estate in 2008.

- MJ sold Neverland in 2008 to help pay his debts. Thereafter, he still had a stake in the property, although how much was never disclosed.

- In March 2009, Michael held a press conference at London's O2 Arena to announce a series of ten comeback/farewell concerts titled "This Is It." According to the promoter, the shows would earn MJ about $80 million. Concerts were also planned for Paris, New York, and Mumbai.

March 5, 2009: Michael addressed the media and some 2,000 fans at London's O2 Arena to announce his forthcoming series of farewell concerts. "This is it," he told them. "This is the final curtain call. See you in July."

"It's an adventure. **It's a great adventure.** We want to take them places that they've never been before. We want to show them talent like they've never seen before."

—Michael Jackson, in the movie This Is It

SPOTLIGHT ON

This Is It

- *After the ten London shows that Michael referred to as his "final curtain call" sold out instantly, the number of concerts was increased to 50, and more than one million tickets were purchased in mere hours.*

- *The concerts were scheduled to take place between July 13, 2009, and March 6, 2010.*

- *Rehearsals for the show were held at L.A.'s Staples Center, where Michael rehearsed moves choreographed by Kenny Ortega with his musicians and dancers.*

- *Following MJ's death just 18 days before the date of the first concert, Columbia Pictures used film of the rehearsals and behind-the-scenes footage to produce a feature-length documentary titled Michael Jackson's This Is It.*

- *Directed by Ortega and initially limited to a two-week theatrical run (from October 28 to November 12, 2009), which was soon extended, This Is It grossed $23 million in the United States alone during its opening weekend. Its theatrical-run earnings of*

$260.8 million worldwide subsequently made it the highest-grossing documentary or concert movie of all time.

■ The movie was released on DVD and Blu-ray in North America on January 26, 2010, and sold a record-breaking 1.5 million units during its first week.

■ A two-disc This Is It compilation album was issued on October 26, 2009, to coincide with the theatrical release of the movie. In addition to 14 already-released tracks, there were album and orchestral versions of "This Is It"; MJ's demo recordings of "She's Out of My Life," "Wanna Be Startin' Somethin'," and "Beat It"; and his spoken-word poem "Planet Earth." It debuted at No. 1 in 14 countries, including the United States, the United Kingdom, and Japan.

Although there were widespread reports of Michael being extremely frail in the leadup to his planned concert tour, these were refuted by his vigorous appearance in the posthumously released documentary, This Is It. Here, he is seen rehearsing on June 23, 2009, just two days before his death.

Gone Too Soon

- *Michael Jackson died on June 25, 2009, at a mansion he was renting at 100 North Carolwood Drive in the Holmby Hills neighborhood of Los Angeles.*

- *He went into cardiac arrest after his personal physician, Dr. Conrad Murray, gave him the powerful anesthetic propofol to help him sleep.*

- *When Dr. Murray failed to resuscitate Michael, L.A. Fire Department paramedics received a 911 call at 12:22 P.M. PST. They arrived at the house three minutes later and, when they saw he wasn't breathing, performed CPR.*

- *Resuscitation efforts continued while Michael was being transported to the Ronald Reagan UCLA Medical Center and for an hour thereafter. He was pronounced dead at 2:26 P.M.*

- *On August 28, 2009, the Los Angeles County Coroner announced that Michael's death was being treated as a homicide. On February 8, 2010, Dr. Murray was charged with involuntary manslaughter.*

- *Michael was laid to rest in a private ceremony at Forest Lawn Memorial Park in Glendale, California, on September 3, 2009.*

Dr. Conrad Murray (right) was charged with manslaughter after having fatally sedated Michael at the $38 million Holmby Hills mansion (above) that MJ was renting for $100,000 a month.

Fan Reaction Around the World

From Detroit (opposite, bottom) to Hollywood (left) to Paris (opposite, top), fans around the world held vigils and paid tribute to the King of Pop.

News Web sites crashed, as did AOL Instant Messenger, due to Web traffic increasing by as much as 20 percent immediately following Michael Jackson's death. Then, as reports and retrospectives consumed the TV and radio broadcast airwaves, people around the world took to the streets to convey their grief and sympathy over an unnecessary and tragic loss, as well as to celebrate one of the greatest artists of their age.

Headlines

Not for nothing was Michael the subject of two weeks of nonstop front-page headlines following his untimely death. This story had everything: drama, mystery, tragedy, outrage, and at its center the world's biggest star—who was about to become the best-selling artist of 2009, shifting more than 31 million albums worldwide.

The shocking news of MJ's death filled newspaper and magazine front pages for several weeks and swamped reports about the passing of iconic actress Farrah Fawcett.

Tributes

"I am so very sad and confused with every emotion possible. I am heartbroken for his children, who I know were everything to him, and for his family. This is such a massive loss on so many levels, words fail me."

—Lisa Marie Presley

"I've lost my little brother today, and part of my soul has gone with him."

—Quincy Jones

"Michael Jackson showed me that you can actually see the beat. He made the music come to life. He made me believe in magic."

—Sean "Diddy" Combs

Michael Jackson influenced and impacted so many people. These included high-profile figures such as his ex-wife Lisa Marie Presley (left); the Reverend Al Sharpton (center); and movie director Steven Spielberg (right).

"The incomparable Michael Jackson has made a bigger impact on music than any other artist in the history of music. He was magic. He was what we all strive to be."

—*Beyoncé*

"Michael Jackson made culture accept a person of color way before Tiger Woods, way before Oprah Winfrey, way before Barack Obama."

—*Reverend Al Sharpton*

"My heart, my mind are broken. I loved Michael with all my soul, and I can't imagine life without him. . . . He will live in my heart forever, but it's not enough. My life feels so empty."

—*Elizabeth Taylor*

"I feel privileged to have hung out and worked with Michael. He was a massively talented boy-man with a gentle soul. His music will be remembered forever, and my memories of our time together will be happy ones."

—*Sir Paul McCartney*

"Just as there will never be another Fred Astaire or Chuck Berry or Elvis Presley, there will never be anyone comparable to Michael Jackson. His talent, his wonderment, and his mystery make him a legend."

—*Steven Spielberg*

"I can't stop crying over the sad news. I have always admired Michael Jackson. The world has lost one of the greats, but his music will live on forever."

—*Madonna*

Public Memorial

- Following a private family service inside Forest Lawn Memorial Park's Hall of Liberty on July 7, 2009, a public memorial was held at L.A.'s Staples Center. Michael's casket was present.

- The memorial featured musical performances by Mariah Carey, Stevie Wonder, Lionel Richie, John Mayer, Jennifer Hudson, Usher, and Jermaine Jackson; Berry Gordy and Smokey Robinson delivered eulogies.

- The Reverend Al Sharpton also paid tribute, and Queen Latifah read a poem written especially for the occasion by Maya Angelou.

- An estimated 31.1 million American TV viewers watched the event, and the worldwide audience was unofficially estimated at more than one billion people.

opposite *MJ's mother Katherine sat between his children Paris and Prince at the public memorial service.* above *Jackson brothers Marlon, Jermaine, and Tito were among the pallbearers.*

"Ever since I was born, Daddy has been the best father you could ever imagine, and I just wanted to say I love him so much."

—Paris Jackson, at MJ's memorial service, July 7, 2009

clockwise from left Paris, Prince, and Blanket, all appeared onstage at the Staples Center during the public memorial for their father.

MJ's Autopsy Report

- *Michael Jackson suffered from vitiligo, which had caused his skin to lose pigmentation.*
- *The hair on his head was "sparse and connected to a wig."*
- *He had tattooed black eyeliner and pink-tattooed lips.*

Michael was laid to rest in the Grand Mausoleum at Forest Lawn Memorial Park in Glendale, California.

- *At the time of his death, he was suffering from numerous ailments, including "chronic lung inflammation, respiratory bronchiolitis, diffuse congestion, and patchy hemorrhage of right and left lungs."*
- *Among the drugs detected in his bloodstream were lidocaine, diazepam, nordiazepam, lorazepam, midazolam, and ephedrine.*

Carrying the Torch

Michael's legacy lives on not only in his own music but also in that of the artists who were profoundly influenced by him. These include such top entertainers as Usher, Beyoncé, Ne-Yo, Rihanna, Justin Timberlake, and Chris Brown, who have not only benefited from MJ's inspiring songwriting, singing, and dancing talents but also his business sense and ability to break down racial barriers.

R&B star Usher performing beside his idol's casket during MJ's public memorial service.

top Chris Brown paying tribute to MJ at the 2006 World Music Awards ceremony at Earl's Court in London. right Beyoncé presenting the King of Pop with a humanitarian award during the Radio Music Awards show at the Aladdin Hotel in Las Vegas in October 2003.

GRAMMY AWARDS

Year	Award	Song/Album
1980	Best Male R&B Vocal	"Don't Stop 'til You Get Enough"
1984	Album of the Year	*Thriller*
	Record of the Year	"Beat It"
	Producer of the Year	*Thriller* (with Quincy Jones)
	Best R&B Song	"Billie Jean"
	Best Recording for Children	"Someone in the Dark"
	Best Male Pop Vocal	"Thriller"
	Best Male R&B Vocal	"Billie Jean"
	Best Male Rock Vocal	"Beat It"

Michael, standing beside record producer Quincy Jones, tries to hold onto the eight Thriller-related Grammy Awards that he won at L.A.'s Shrine Auditorium on February 28, 1984.

Year	Award	Song/Album
1985	Best Long Form Video	*The Making of "Thriller"*
1986	Song of the Year	"We Are the World" (with Lionel Richie)
	Record of the Year	"We Are the World"
	Best Pop Performance by a Duo or Group with Vocal	"We Are the World"
	Best Short Form Music Video	"We Are the World"
1988	Best Performance Music Video	"The Way You Make Me Feel"
1990	Best Short Form Music Video	"Leave Me Alone"
1993	Living Legend Award	
1996	Best Short Form Music Video	"Scream"
2010	Grammy Lifetime Achievement Award	

Top of the Pops

- *Thriller is the best-selling album of all time, having spent a record 80 consecutive weeks in the Top Ten of the Billboard Hot 100.*
- *Five of Michael's albums—* Bad, Dangerous, HIStory, Invincible, *and* Michael Jackson's This Is It—*all debuted atop the Billboard 200.*
- *Off the Wall was the first album to spawn four Top Ten U.S. singles, and* Thriller *was the first to produce seven of them.*
- *MJ is the only artist to have scored five chart-topping U.S. singles off one album (Bad).*

Among Michael Jackson's many, many recorded achievements, Thriller *is the work for which he'll always be best remembered.*

- Thriller *and "Billie Jean" made Michael the first artist to have the number one album and single on* Billboard*'s pop and R&B charts at the same time.*

- *"You Are Not Alone" was the first single to debut atop the* Billboard Hot 100.

- *In 2009, MJ became the first-ever artist to have four of the Top 20 best-selling albums in the United States within a single year.*

- *MJ's 13* Billboard Hot 100 *chart toppers place him just behind The Beatles (20), Mariah Carey (18), and Elvis Presley (18). With USA for Africa's "We Are the World" and The Jackson 5's four No. 1 singles, his total climbs to 18.*

- *MJ's 28 Top Ten hits on the* Billboard Hot 100 *have him trailing Madonna (37), Elvis Presley (36), and The Beatles (29).*

"Billie Jean" featured the iconic Michael Jackson on record, on video, and definitely onstage.

"If you enter this world knowing you are loved and you leave this world knowing the same, then everything that happens in between can be dealt with."

—Michael Jackson,
Dancing the Dream: Poems and Reflections

"Did you ever stop to notice the crying Earth, the weeping shores..." At the 1996 World Music Awards show in Monte Carlo, Michael addressed his concerns over the environment, animal welfare, disadvantaged children, and the future of the world with a moving performance of "Earth Song."

Index

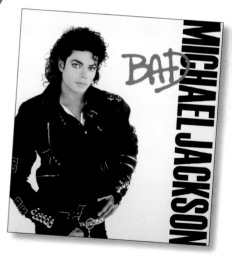

Photo credits:

Front cover: Getty Images; Shutterstock.com (background)

Back cover: NFL; Shutterstock.com (background)

Alamy Images: Photos-12, 175; **AP Images:** 10 (left), 35, 45 (top), 57, 71, 73 (right), 104, 146, 148–49, 154, 185 (left), 187, 194, 197, 199, 202, 207, 209, 227 (bottom), 231, 232 (right), 245, 249, 258, 259, 261 (bottom), 266, 267, 270, 271, 283, 285 (left), 288, 295 (top), 300 (left, right & center), 307 (bottom), 308; Paul Drinkwater/NBCU Photo Bank, 179, 180, 181; Sipa, 305; **Corbis:** Tammie Arroy/AFF/Retna Ltd., 8, 52 (top); Bettmann, 33, 53 (top), 63, 69, 185 (right); Gene Blevins/*LA Daily-News,* 295 (bottom); John Bryson/Sygma, 147; Stephane Cardinale, 313; Stephane Cardinale/People Avenue, 307 (top); dpa, 290; Najlah Feanny, 241; Lynn Goldsmith, 159; Jeff Kowalsky/epa, 53 (bottom); Rick Maiman/Sygma, 250; Robert Matheu/Retna Ltd., 157; Michael Ochs Archives, 48 (bottom); Hamad Mohammed/Reuters, 289; Pool Photos/Retna Ltd., 303, 306; Neal Preston, 88, 234 (left); Nina Prommer/epa, 273; Reuters, 272, 278; Jacqueline Sallow, 191; Steve Starr, 227 (top); STR/epa, 291; YONHAP/epa, 229; **Courtesy Heritage Auctions:** 10 (right), 29 (top right & bottom left), 48 (left & top right), 83, 103 (right), 143, 201, 225, 235; **Dustin Drase Collection:** 74, 107, 151, 156, 162, 166, 167, 170, 211, 237, 311, 316, 317; **Getty Images:** 11 (left & right), 18, 20, 21, 28, 32, 75, 93, 99, 100, 113, 125, 127, 139, 165 (right), 173, 189, 212, 234 (right), 240, 242 (bottom left), 246, 261 (top), 275, 293, 297 (bottom), 302, 304; AFP, 153, 254, 255, 269, 296, 297 (top); Contour, 277; Michael Ochs Archives, 7, 9, 17, 22, 29 (top left & bottom right), 31, 36, 41, 47, 49 (top & bottom), 54, 59, 60, 78, 81, 85, 91, 101, 105, 110 (left & right), 112, 119, 131, 144, 160, 232 (left), 263 (left); *NY Daily News,* 39, 50; Sankei Archive, 281; Time Life Pictures, 13, 87, 219 (top left); **Judson Picco Collection:** 135, 141; **Library of Congress:** 103 (left); **NFL:** 247; **Photofest:** 217, 310; **PIL Collection:** title page, contents, 25, 26 (left & right), 27 (left & right), 44, 45 (bottom), 46, 66 (left & right), 67 (top & bottom), 73 (left), 76, 77 (left & right), 80, 84, 90, 94 (left & right), 95, 96, 102, 106, 109, 111, 114, 117, 118, 123, 129 (top & bottom), 132, 133, 140, 145 (left & right), 161, 168 (left & right), 169 (left & right), 172 (top & bottom), 176–77, 196, 204, 205, 206, 215 (top & bottom), 223, 239, 257, 265, 268, 274, 276 (top & bottom), 287, 298, 299 (top & bottom), 314, 315, 318, 319; **Redferns:** contents, 5, 14, 15, 61, 64, 65, 97, 115, 121, 136, 152, 183, 193, 263 (right); **Ron Seymour/Levrecht Music & Arts:** The Image Works, 43; **Shutterstock.com:** 155 (top left, right & bottom left); **U.S. Patent Office:** 219 (right); **WireImage:** 10 (center), 19, 52 (bottom), 72, 158, 165 (left), 171, 188, 198, 221, 233, 242 (top & bottom right), 243, 253, 279, 280; **ZUMA Press:** © Entertainment Pictures, 219 (bottom left); Globe Photos, 285 (right)